God, the Holy Spirit

be a conductor of his power

Enoch Adejare Adeboye

An imprint of Pneuma Life Publishing
Largo, MD

Copyright © 2002 Enoch Adejare Adeboye

Christian Living Books, Inc.
An imprint of Pneuma Life Publishing, Inc.
P. O. Box 7584
Largo, MD 20792
301-218-9092
www.christianlivingbooks.com

ISBN 0-9711760-1-9

Printed in the United States of America

contents

preface

Many Christians feel frustrated, defeated and fruitless. Many are wallowing in spiritual poverty, unaware of the great resources of God available to them. However, the wonderful truth is that every Christian has the potential to live supernaturally. The key is God, the Holy Spirit. He is the Commander-in-Chief of the army of Christ. He is the Lord of the harvest. He is the Highest in revival, evangelism and every Christian endeavor.

If you do not have the Holy Spirit, you are a sub-normal Christian. You are a second-class citizen of Heaven on earth. You are the living dead. If you have the Holy Spirit, then you are a first-class Christian of the supernatural realm.

The Holy Spirit is the secret of the supernatural, the secret behind healing miracles. He is the word of knowledge, prophecy and the discerning of spirits. If you want to know tomorrow, get the Holy Spirit. If you want miracles to happen in your ministry, get the Holy Spirit. If you want to live a successful Christian life, get the Holy Spirit. Without Him you are useless, but with Him, you will be a wonderful and unforgettable person.

— Pastor E. A. Adeboye

chapter 1

the original comforter

And I will ask the Father and he will give you another Counselor to be with you forever—the Spirit of Truth. The world cannot accept him because it neither sees him nor knows him. But you know him, for he lives in you and will be in you. I will not leave you as orphans; I will come to you. (John 14:16-18)

"another comforter" implies there was an original comforter

In the Scripture above, as Jesus Christ made his exit, He said He would ask the Father to give us another Comforter who will abide with us forever. "Another comforter" implies there was a Comforter before: Jesus Christ Himself.

We love to talk about Jesus: He is our savior, our healer. However, when you are talking about the Holy Spirit, you are talking about Jesus Christ, too. God the Holy Trinity is one.

1

Now there was a man in Jerusalem called Simeon, who
was righteous and devout. He was waiting for the con-
solation of Israel and the Holy Spirit was upon him.

(Luke 2:25)

Simeon was waiting for Jesus Christ, the One called the consola-
tion of Israel. He is also called the bright and morning star, the
sun of righteousness. He is the one who brings light into darkness.
(2 Peter 1:19) When people mourn, they wear dark clothes. But
when the light of God's comfort comes in, darkness departs and
light overrules darkness.

The people walking in darkness have seen a great light;
on those living in the land of the shadow of death a
light has dawned. (Isaiah 9:2)

Who is the light of the world? Jesus Christ. (2 Corinthians 4:4,6)
When He was here, wherever He went, He brought comfort. When
Jesus went to the house of Jairus, the first thing He did was to ban-
ish the sounds of sorrow from the professional mourners he met
there. Then he gave life to the one that was dead and said the child
should be fed. Jesus Christ is the bread of life. Whenever He comes
in, sorrow leaves and people are filled with joy. Whenever Jesus
comes in, death and hunger depart. He was, and is, the Comforter.

To a sick man, comfort can only come when he gets well. Comfort
comes to the hungry person only when he is fed. And to someone
who has lost a loved one, comfort can come when the dead is
raised. When Jesus saw the widow of Nain going to bury her only
son, He had compassion on her and raised the boy. As He
approached the city of Jericho, He saw a blind beggar by the road-
side that begged for mercy healing. Jesus had the compassion to
heal the man.

All those who came to Jesus received solutions to their problems.
When a leper came to Him to be made clean, Jesus made him
clean. The leper went home rejoicing and comforted. In Mark
5:25-34 we read of a woman who was not only bleeding to death

but whose twelve-year-long medical bills had reversed her fortunes. She touched the hem of Jesus' garment and went home comforted because she was healed, and she never had to spend money on medical bills again. I assure you that if you are ill and you come to Jesus Christ, your medical bills will become history, in Jesus' name.

Another woman came to Jesus with a demon-possessed daughter. Though He was not particularly polite to her, she persisted with a humble heart, determined not to go home until her problem was solved. Jesus did solve the problem. (Matthew 15:22-28)

The Holy spirit is called the spirit of christ

> *You are controlled by the Spirit of God if He lives in you. Those who do not have the Spirit of Christ are controlled by their sinful nature, and do not belong to Christ.* (Romans 8:9)

The Holy Spirit behaves exactly like Jesus Christ, since Jesus is here as the Holy Spirit. We may not be able to see Him but we can feel Him. Jesus Christ made it clear to us that the Holy Spirit moves with the wind:

> *The wind blows wherever it pleases. You hear its sound but you cannot tell where it comes from or where it is going. So it is with everyone born of the Spirit.*
> (John 3:8)

You cannot see Jesus Christ face-to-face until his return, but I am happy to tell you that the Holy Spirit is near you. If you are a child of God, you can never be alone. The Comforter is with you forever. By providing another Comforter, Jesus Christ was making up for many of the things He could not do because He had to go back to Heaven to seal our relationship with God. Jesus said He would send someone exactly like Himself, another Comforter, who would do exactly what He would have done. He sent the Holy Spirit.

I thank God that Jesus went home. I thank God that the Holy Spirit has come. Jesus Christ said the Holy Spirit would come and stay with us, and live in us permanently. When God wants to talk to you, He speaks through the Holy Spirit who is already within you. No one can hear the conversation—it's private and confidential between you and your Father.

The word "comforter" can also be translated as "instructor," "teacher," "monitor" or "advocate." When we say the Holy Spirit is the instructor, we know that Jesus Christ Himself was the teacher.

> *Jesus said to her "Mary." She turned toward him and cried out in Aramaic, "Rabboni"* [which means teacher]. (John 20:16)

"Rabboni" means the teacher of teachers. He was called "rabbi" in Matthew 23:7-8.

> *Finally the temple guards went back to the chief priests and Pharisees who asked them, "Why didn't you bring him in?" "No one ever spoke the way this man does,"* the guards declared. (John 7: 45-46)

Nobody can teach like Jesus Christ, but the other Comforter that Jesus Christ promised us will be a teacher and rabboni. He will be an Instructor in the mysteries of God, revealing the deep meanings of the word of God. With Him to instruct you, you do not need the earthly words of human wisdom. There are several passages in the Bible that are difficult to understand. Your pastor may not even be able to help you, but the Holy Spirit will decode such sections in details if you go to Him.

When I was a new believer, I had many questions to which I needed answers. For example, I wanted to know why God planted the tree of the forbidden fruit in the Garden of Eden when He knew that Adam and Eve would eat the fruit. Then when they ate the fruit, why did He get angry with them? You often cannot ask a pastor this type of question—particularly years ago when I became born again. But I asked the Holy Spirit and He gave me answers that satisfied me completely. If you want answers to questions no one has been able to deal with, ask the Holy Spirit and He will help you.

The Holy Spirit is also called the captain, a kind of overseer watching over you, leading you and assisting you when necessary. If you follow the Holy Spirit, you will never go astray.

Jesus Christ said:

> *I have much to say to you more than you can now bear. But when He the Spirit of Truth comes He will guide you into all Truth. He will not speak on his own; He will speak only what He hears and He will tell you what is yet to come. He will bring glory to me by taking from what is mine and making it known to you.*
>
> (John 16:12-14)

Here, Jesus is simply telling us that the Holy Spirit will be our captain. He will point the way. You should take your directions from the Him; he will tell you where to go and where not to go.

> *Those who are led by the Spirit of God are the sons of God.* (Romans 8:14)

Who should guide the children of God? The Holy Spirit is to be our leader. He is willing and able to tell you who to marry, who not to marry, who to work with and who not to work with.

God wants you to live a supernatural kind of life. When I first received the Holy Spirit, anytime I would leave home for church, the Holy Spirit would tell me who would preach, who would pray and the songs we would sing. God is no respecter of persons: what He can do for me, He can do for you. If you have the Holy Spirit, nobody will be able to deceive you. You will know many things that are not common knowledge.

Ananias and Sapphira came to Peter and lied to him about the price of the land they sold. Peter was not with them when they sold the land, but he knew they lied about it. So he simply said they had deceived the Holy Spirit and this led to their deaths—fear killed them!

When you have the Holy Spirit, you will succeed in your business ventures because the Holy Spirit will tell you what investments are good or bad. He will give you insights into the future.

The Holy Spirit is also called the advocate, a word that can also be interpreted as "lawyer." A lawyer can work for you or against you; they can represent either the prosecution or the defense. The Holy Spirit is always witnessing to sinners about the truth of God and sinners' sinfulness. He pleads against a dead conscience convicting a sinner of his sins, but He also pleads for the saints before God, with unimaginably deep emotional intensity.

If a sinner loves to drink alcohol, the Holy Spirit impresses upon him that it could create an addiction, which could be fatal to his future. If a sinner says he wants to live for himself rather than yield his life to Christ, the Holy Spirit reminds him that his life is not his own—it belongs to the Lord of life, Jesus Christ. If a sinner says he will submit to the Lordship of Jesus Christ when he gets old, the Holy Spirit recounts the history of a person who died young and without Jesus. If you are not yet born again, you must surrender to Jesus today for your soul to be saved.

As a child of God, the Holy Spirit advocates for you. He perfects your prayer as He pleads for you before God. In the same way, the Spirit helps us in our weakness. We often do not know what we ought to pray for, but the Spirit himself intercedes for us with groans that words cannot express. (Romans 8:26) The Holy Spirit goes before God, pleading for you. When He prays for you, you always get what you want.

The Holy Spirit is a faithful, wise, true and loving Comforter. He knows how to lovingly strengthen you. Often people who want to comfort you end up doing more harm than good. When you are grieving, the Holy Spirit soothes your sorrows away. Surely you need Him now.

chapter 2

seek the holy spirit

There are different kinds of gifts but the same Spirit. Now to each one the manifestation of the Spirit is given for the common good. And these are the work of one and the same Spirit and he gives them to each one just as he determines. (1 Corinthians 12:4,7,11)

To seek the holy spirit is to seek god

Who is the Holy Spirit? Some people think He is the power of God. Others think He is something you cannot describe. The Bible says:

How much more then will the blood of Christ, who through the eternal spirit offered himself unblemished to God, cleanse our consciences from acts that lead to death so that we may serve the living God?

(Hebrews 9:14)

The Bible refers to the Holy Spirit as eternal, having no beginning and no end. David said:

Where can I go from your spirit? Where can I flee from your presence? (Psalm 139:7)

The Holy Spirit is always everywhere:

However, as it is written; no eye has seen, no ear has heard, no mind has conceived what God has prepared for those who love him. But God has revealed it to us by his spirit. The spirit searches all things, even the deep things of God. For who among men knows the thoughts of a man, except the man's spirit within him? In the same way, no one knows the thoughts of God except the spirit of God. (1 Corinthians 2:9-11)

The Holy Spirit knows all things, including the hidden wisdom of God:

The Angel answered, The Holy Spirit will come upon you and the power of the Most High will overshadow you. So the holy one to be born will be called the Son of God. (Luke 1:35)

The Holy Spirit has all powers, including those of the Most High. The verse above is just another way of saying that the Holy Spirit is God Almighty Himself. No other is eternal, omnipresent, omniscient and omnipotent. By learning more about the Holy Spirit, we are learning more about God. By seeking the Holy Spirit, we are seeking God.

How you spend eternity could be determined by your response to the Holy spirit

If all that we have learned so far is what the Holy Spirit is, then how do people respond to Him?

Then Peter said, Ananais, how is it that Satan has so filled your heart that you have lied to the Holy Spirit and have kept for yourself some of the money you received for the land? (Acts 5:3)

One way people respond is by lying to the Holy Spirit—a suicidal, surefire subway to an especially horrid part of Hell. There are many ways we lie to the Holy Spirit. One is to claim the baptism of the Holy Spirit when you have not really been baptized. Another way is to speak in tongues claiming utterance by the Holy Spirit when you know you are demon-possessed; the devil also has his way of speaking in deceptive tongues. But by far the most widespread falsehood is lying to a man of God.

Others respond to the Holy Spirit by resisting Him. One example is refusing to yield your tongue to Him:

You stiff-necked people with uncircumcised hearts and ears! You are just like your fathers; you always resist the Holy Spirit! (Acts 7:51)

When you resist God, you ask for trouble. Some have grieved Him through deliberate sins, resistance or disobedience.

And do not grieve the Holy Spirit of God with whom you were sealed for the day of redemption.
                                        (Ephesians 4:30)

If you discourage or despise anyone filled with the Holy Spirit, you are against Him. Some have even insulted the Holy Spirit or blasphemed Him, thus permanently closing the door of Heaven against themselves.

How much more severely do you think a man deserves to be punished who has trample the Son of God under foot, who has treated as an unholy thing the blood of the covenant that sanctified him and who has insulted the Spirit of Grace? (Hebrews 10:29)

And so I tell you every sin and blasphemy will be forgiven men, but the blasphemy against the Spirit will not be forgiven. (Matthew 12:31)

If you revile the Holy Spirit, your eternal reward will be damnation. Jesus said if you offend God the Father and God the Son you can be forgiven, but if you offend God the Holy Spirit you are damned forever. So any time the Holy Spirit shows up and strange things happen, if you do not understand, keep your mouth shut.

Do not put out the Spirit's fire. (1 Thessalonians 5:19)

Some have quenched the fire and light of the Holy Spirit in their lives, but if you always obey the Holy Spirit, you will discover that His power will grow in you. He will use you more and more. If you reject Him, His power in you will be withdrawn. Instead of resisting the Holy Spirit, lying to Him, despising, grieving and profaning His name, you can obey Him and you will be blessed for it.

if you listen you can hear his voice

We have learned that the Holy Spirit helps us in prayer, teaches us and guides us. He convicts sinners and backsliders, and witnesses for and of Jesus Christ. The Holy Spirit can also give commands. How? He speaks.

He who has an ear, let him hear what the Spirit says to the churches. To him who overcomes, I will give the right to eat from the tree of life which is in the paradise of God. (Revelation 2:7)

The Holy Spirit is the One who speaks to the Churches. It is our duty to learn how to hear Him. To do so, your spiritual ear must be open. However, His first words to you may be a command:

While they were worshipping the Lord and they were fasting the Holy Spirit said, "Set apart for me Barnabas

and Saul for the work to which I have called them.
(Acts 13:2)

The Holy Spirit gave them a command. If you are willing, He will instruct you. When He guides you, you will never go astray—that is, if you obey Him.

HE IS willing if you are

What is the Holy Spirit willing to do for you today? Titus tells you about one of His acts:

He saved us not because of righteous things we have done but because of His mercy. He saved us through the washing of rebirth and renewal by the Holy Spirit. (Titus 3:5)

He is willing to renew you. If you have lost His power in your life, seek Him again.

The Holy Spirit is willing to reside in you and seal you so you will be recognized as Jesus Christ's possession. If the Holy Spirit of God marks you as His possession, you have a spiritual identification instantly recognized by all opposition, so they avoid you. When you are sealed, you are clothed with Christ.

> *For all of you who are baptized into Christ have clothed yourselves with Christ. There is neither Jew nor Greek, slave nor free, male nor female, for you are all one in Christ Jesus. If you belong to Christ then you are Abraham's seed and heirs according to the promise.*
> (Galatians 3:27-29)

The Holy Spirit is ready to fuse you into the Body of Christ through baptism, and with baptism comes God's power.

The Holy Spirit also wants to perform miracles for you. Acts 8:29 tells us about the Spirit's directives to Philip. Once Philip obeyed Him, the Holy Spirit did something spectacular:

god, the Holy spirit

When they came up out of the water, the Spirit of the Lord suddenly took Philip away and the Eunuch did not see him again but went on his way rejoicing.

(Acts 8:39)

The Holy Spirit supernaturally transported Philip from the wilderness. This "Philip Air Express" experience can still happen today because the Holy Spirit is the same now and forever.

chapter 3

the holy spirit speaks

Undoubtedly there are all sorts of languages in the world, yet none of them is without meaning.

(1 Corinthians 14:10)

Here we can interpret "languages" as "voices," and indeed there are all sorts of voices in this world. How can we differentiate the voice of God from the rest? Perhaps we should approach this using the theory of elimination. Let's identify all other voices that are *not* of God. That is, let's start by identifying the voice of the devil.

The Devil speaks in Two principal ways

We all hear voices, whether it is the voice of God or that of the devil. Even if you are not a born-again Christian, you can still hear the voices of conscience or lust. Some people hear the voice of the devil constantly; many insane people are under the full deluge of the devil's voice without relief.

The devil speaks in two principal ways. He can talk in a small voice to the spirit of Man, and he can talk through human beings. He can speak to your spirit in your dreams, sometimes disguised as an angel of light. For example, he may appear as the likeness of your mother-in-law who dislikes you. When you wake up in the morning, the tendency will be to have a face-off with your mother-in-law, but in actual fact the devil set you up.

A very good example of how the devil can sneak up on you is found in Luke 2:1-7. The devil knew that Jesus Christ was about to come into the world. He was aware that the angel Gabriel appeared to Mary, and he heard everything that Gabriel told her. So he planned to kill Jesus even before He was born. He knew when Mary would give birth to her child and that Joseph would have to travel with her because of the census. The devil expected Mary to deliver the Baby Jesus on the road without medical attention—but as we know, God is wiser than the devil.

It was the plan of the devil that Jesus would die before He could become what God had purposed for Him. The devil talked Herod into the decree issued to kill all children younger than two years of age in the hope that Jesus would be killed too.

If you are a man of God, the devil particularly prefers to speak to you in the second way, which is through human beings.

Now Sarai, Abram's wife had borne him no children. But she had an Egyptian maidservant named Hagar; So she said to Abram, "The Lord has kept me from having children. Go, sleep with my maidservant; perhaps I can build a family through her." Abram agreed to what Sarai said. So after Abraham had been living in Canaan ten years, Sarai his wife took her Egyptian maidservant Hagar and gave her to her husband to be his wife. He slept with Hagar and she conceived. When she knew she was pregnant, she began to despise her mistress. Then Sarai said to Abram, "You are responsible for the wrong I am suffering. I put my servant in your arms and now that she knows she is pregnant she despises me. May the Lord judge between you and me."

"Your servant is in your hands" Abram said. "Do with her whatever you think best." Then Sarai mistreated Hagar so she fled from her. (Genesis 16:1-6)

The devil spoke through Sarah. The political problems confronting Israel today stem from the fact that Abraham listened to her. If the devil had approached Abraham and told him to take another wife, he would have refused, knowing that it was not the voice of God.

In Job we have another example. Job was very close to God, and the devil knew this so he did not talk to him directly. He went through his wife:

His wife said to him, "Are you still holding on to your integrity? Curse God and die!" (Job 2:9)

Be assured that I am not saying anytime your wife speaks to you, it's really the devil speaking. My point is that you make sure that any advice from anyone agrees with the word of God. When Satan can't get to you directly, he likes using those you love, whose advice you are likely to accept.

We have another example in Matthew 16:21-23. Jesus had just finished talking with His disciples about who people thought He was. They told Him that some people thought He was John the Baptist, some thought He was Elias or Jeremiah and some thought He was one of the prophets. Jesus then asked them whom they thought He was. Peter said He was the Christ, the son of the living God. Jesus praised Peter for listening to Heaven. But then:

From that time on Jesus began to explain to his disciples that he must go to Jerusalem and suffer many things at the hands of the elders, chief priests and teachers of the law and that he must be killed and on the third day be raised to life. Peter took him aside and began to rebuke him, "Never Lord!" he said. "This shall never happen to you!" Jesus turned and said to Peter,

"Get behind me, Satan! You are a stumbling block to me; you do not have in mind the things of God, but the things of men." (Matthew 16:21-23)

After Peter heard from God, he also heard from the devil and tried to be his spokesman. The devil knew that Jesus Christ had yet to receive strength from His Father for the journey to the cross. The devil stepped in by using Peter, possessing him to attempt to counter Jesus' willingness to carry out His father's will even if it involved death. However, Jesus was familiar with the voice of the devil. You too should also be able to recognize and reject the devil's voice.

god speaks in Diverse ways

God can speak in a still, small voice. He spoke to Elijah in a mild whisper:

After the earthquake came a fire, but the Lord was not in the fire. And after the fire came a gentle whisper.
(1 Kings 19:12)

After you become born-again and your spirit has been recreated, God can speak to your spirit. He can also speak to you through human beings, particularly through His own prophets. He does this when your inner spiritual ear has been deafened by sin. You may begin to hear from God today if you forsake all your sins, but if there is sin in your life, you will not hear Him. If you are washed in the Blood and there is no sin blocking your channel of communication with God, you can hear Him loud and clear.

David provides an example. When David was anointed, the Bible tells us that he started prophesying. You cannot prophesy if you do not hear from God. Before David waged wars, he asked God first and God answered him. However, from the moment David sinned, he could no longer hear God. When David's spiritual ear went dead, God had to send the prophet Nathan to David to convict him of his sin with Bathsheba. (2 Samuel 12:1-12) Sin had made David insensitive to God.

The same thing happened to Eli, a prophet of God. He failed to reprimand his children, Hophni and Phinehas, who carried out sacrilegious acts in the Temple. To get to him, God had to talk to little Samuel. (1 Samuel 3:11-18) Samuel had never heard from God before so he thought it was Eli speaking, but Eli knew that it was God who spoke to Samuel because he was familiar with God's style of communication.

If you understand the things of God, you would have realized by now that sin is dangerous to a believer. If you sin, God will cut the link between Him and you. It is my prayer that the Spirit of God will never leave you.

Another example is King Saul, who heard from Heaven and prophesied when anointed as king. Then he sinned and could no longer hear God, so God had to make Samuel the go-between. Sin is the one major reason that cuts off the link between you and God. When God sends someone to you, that person is most likely to deliver the judgment of God or give you a warning.

There are other ways in which God can speak. When you are too busy to listen to the still, small voice of God or you doubt His prophet, He will come to you face-to-face. This is always very powerful. Moses' encounter with God in the desert is a case in point. If God had sent a prophet to tell Moses that he was to deliver the children of Israel, Moses would never have believed him. He would have told the prophet that he became a murderer at his first attempt at the job. He would have told the prophet that God had forgotten him.

> *Now Moses was tending the flock of Jethro his father-in-law, the priest of Midian and he led the flock to the far side of the desert and came to Horeb, the mountain of God. There the angel of the Lord appeared to him in a flame of fire from within a bush. Moses saw that though the bush was on fire it did not burn up. So*

Moses thought, "I will go over and see this strange sight – why the bush does not burn up." When the Lord saw that he had gone over to look, God called to him from within the bush, "Moses, Moses!" And Moses said "Here I am." "Do not come any closer, God said. "Take off your sandals, for the place where you are standing is holy ground." Then he said, "I am the God of your father, the God of Abraham, the God of Isaac and the God of Jacob." At this, Moses hid his face, because he was afraid to look at God. The Lord said, "I have indeed seen the misery of my people in Egypt. I have heard them crying out because of their slave drivers and I am concerned about their suffering. So I have come down to rescue them from the hand of the Egyptians and to bring them up out of that land into a good and spacious land, a land flowing with milk and honey—the home of the Canaanites, Hittites, Amorites, Perizzites, Hivites and Jebusites. And now the cry of the Israelites has reached me and I have seen the way the Egyptians are oppressing them. So now go I am sending you to Pharaoh to bring my people the Israelites out of Egypt." But Moses said to God, "Who am I that I should go to Pharaoh and bring the Israelites out of Egypt?" And God said, "I will be with you. And this will be the sign to you that it is I who have sent you: When you have brought the people out of Egypt, you will worship God on this mountain." Moses said to God, "Suppose I go to the Israelites and say to them, "The God of your fathers has sent me to you," and they ask me "What is his name? Then what shall I tell them? God said to Moses, "I AM WHO I AM. This is what you are to say to the Israelites: I AM has sent me to you."

(Exodus 3:1-14)

Even after God spoke directly to Moses in that fire, he still questioned God.

Another example is the story of Joshua at the wall of Jericho and Gideon, when God had to call him to deliver Israel. (Joshua 5:13, 6:5; Judges 6:11-16) And we have a very good example in the story of Saul of Tarsus. Nobody could have preached to get him converted. He thought that he was right and others were wrong, so God knocked him down to make him listen. Had Peter preached to him, Saul would have fed Peter to the lions. There are many people today who will not listen to Jesus until He brings them to their knees.

When time is of the essence, God can speak through any medium, as in the story of Balaam and his donkey. God can use the mouth of an animal to get His message across. He can also speak to you through your children.

Differences between the voice of god and the voice of the devil

How can we differentiate between the voice of God and that of the devil? The voice of the devil always contradicts the voice of God:

> *You belong to your father the devil and you want to carry out your father's desire. He was a murderer from the beginning, not holding to the truth for there is no truth in him. When he lies, he speaks his native language for he is a liar and the father of lies.* (John 8:44)

The devil can never speak the truth, but you have to be very careful because the devil knows the Bible and can quote it. If you are not vigilant, he may deceive you into thinking that God is speaking to you. And if you do not know how to quote the Bible correctly, you will be in trouble. Someone once quoted a Bible passage to me this way: "Heaven helps those who help themselves." So I asked what part of the Bible the passage came from. If you do not know the Bible very well, you would think the statement is accurate because the Bible is always talking about Heaven, but it is not. If you are quoting the Bible as your defense against the devil, make sure you quote it correctly!

This reminds me of the story of some believers who were casting out demons. As they quoted the scripture, "It is written, in the Name of Jesus, every knee shall bow," the demons laughed them to scorn that the believers did not know the Bible by heart. The demons corrected the believers that the Bible states, "At the name of Jesus every knee shall bow." Try to memorize the Bible correctly, because one way God speaks to you as a believer is by referring you to a particular verse in the Bible. We know the voice of God because it agrees with the word of God.

The voice of God frightens sinners. After they sinned, Adam and Eve became afraid when they heard His voice. (Genesis 3:9-10) The voice of the devil encourages you to continue in sin, but the voice of God is a source of joy to believers.

How to Hear God's Voice

After your baptism in the Holy Spirit, God begins to speak to you. It starts as if you have an idea and, usually, it will be a strange idea. But if you apply the idea, you see good results. Once you begin to get these ideas frequently, then you recognize that they are from God. He speaks to your inner mind and, consequently, your thought processes.

The first time God spoke to me, I was heading home from my job as a professor at the university. On the way, I had the idea to take a longer route home. I brushed it off and took the shorter way but soon I came to a traffic jam, where I was stuck for several hours. Eventually I had to take the route I had rejected earlier. When I got home, I knew that that idea was not *just* an idea.

God can speak to you too, but only if you talk to Him. If you want to hear from Him frequently, remember that God is a spirit and those who worship Him must worship Him in spirit and in truth. If you pray in tongues often, you will hear from God often.

If you are a sinner but you want to hear from God, you are deceiving yourself. The first thing you must do is to accept Jesus Christ as your Lord and Savior, and let Him wash you in His Blood. When you have done this, He will go ahead to baptize you in the Holy Spirit and sanctify you. Then will He begin to talk to you.

chapter 4

a holy ghost carrier

the holy spirit wants you to be a conductor of his power

There are two kinds of power: constructive and destructive. Satan continually destroys. God constructs and only destroys when necessary. The Holy Spirit gives life, restores life and destroys the works of the devil wherever they may be found. And therefore, through the Holy Spirit, believers too can construct and destroy. God wants you to be a conductor of His power.

Examples abound in both the Old and New Testaments of men such as Jesus Christ, Moses, Aaron, Joshua, Elijah, Elisha, Peter, Paul and Stephen, who used the power of the Holy Spirit to perform miracles of construction or destruction. The testimonies of Paul indicate that, from time to time, his handkerchiefs healed the sick. The power of God in him was transferred into the handkerchief, which was then laid on the sick and they were healed.

Different types of wire conduct electricity differently. If a wire is not very pure, only little power will travel through it. In the same way, if you want to be a conductor of the power of God, you must be pure.

Choose seven men among you who are known to be full of the Spirit and wisdom. We will turn this responsibility over to them. This proposal pleased the whole group. They chose Stephen, a man full of faith and of the Holy Spirit; also Philip, Procorus, Nicanor, Timon, Parmenas and Nicolas from Antioch, a convert to Judaism. Now Stephen a man, full of faith and power, did great wonders and miracles among the people.

(Acts 6:3,5,8)

I want God to be able to say about me that I am good, full of faith and power, doing great wonders and miracles among the people. If you want God to say the same about you, you must be ready to meet His conditions. The purer you are, the mightier the works you will be able to do for God.

не who нos surrendered нis tongue нos surrendered нis all

We have already said that once you lay hands on people, the power of God will flow through your hands. Our tongue has a great role to play, too.

The tongue has the power of life and death and those who love it will eat its fruits. (Proverbs 18:21)

When we are filled with the Holy Spirit, whatever we say will come to pass:

"Have faith in God" Jesus answered. "I tell you the truth if anyone says to this mountain, 'Go throw yourself into the sea' and does not doubt in his heart but believes that what he says will happen, it will be done for him." (Mark 11:22-23)

In this passage, Jesus had just demonstrated the power of the tongue by cursing a fig tree. It died, to the amazement of His disciples. Jesus had the power of the Holy Spirit working within Him. One of the reasons Jesus Christ never prayed with His disciples was when He prayed, He did so in tongues. At that time the Holy Spirit had not yet come and the disciples would not have understood. It was after such prayers that Jesus was able to heal the sick and perform other miracles. When you speak in tongues, you touch the power of the Almighty God.

Men like Elijah, Elisha and Paul decreed things under the influence of the Holy Spirit and those things were established. Elisha asked God to open the eyes of his servant and at once he was able to see horses and chariots of fire around them. He also asked God to blindfold the Syrian soldiers and instantly they became blind. (This example illustrates the constructive and destructive nature of God's power.) God told Naaman to wash in the Jordan River to be healed of leprosy and as soon as Naaman washed, he became clean. Elisha said there would be no rain and there was no rain. Elijah called fire down from Heaven and it destroyed two captains and their troops immediately.

One's tongue is the switch that makes the power flow or stop flowing.

> We all stumble in many ways. If anyone is never at fault in what he says, he is a perfect man able to keep his whole body in check. When we put bits into the mouths of horses to make them obey us, we can turn the whole animal. (James 3:2-3)

The Holy Spirit insists on taking over your tongue because once He has it, He has you. Those who surrender their all can be a true channel for the power of the Holy Spirit. Consequently, the more you pray in tongues the greater the mighty works you will be able to do for God. This is the secret of those who perform wonders for God: they surrender their tongues to the Holy Spirit.

chapter 5

Remaining powerful

NO LOSS without a cause

If you have lost the power that God has given you, there must be a reason. You must retrace your steps. How did it happen? One thing we must not forget is that God never changes. Therefore, if there is any change, it comes from us. The Bible tells us that the gifts and calling of God are without repentance. This means that once God gives you a particular gift or He gives you a share of His power, He has given it to you forever. He has no intention of taking it away from you, but you can throw it away.

People say prayer changes things, which may be true, but I know for sure that prayer changes people. It doesn't change God; He is the same before you pray, while you are praying, and will be the same after you have finished praying. The moment you realize that you have lost your power, ask yourself: Where did you go wrong? Where did you open the door for the devil to come in?

There are several reasons why you may lose your power, and if you have, the Holy Spirit will tell you why. One main cause is doubt. When God gives you something good, the moment you begin to doubt whether or not it is real, the devil takes it away from you.

After all, you were not really sure that you had it. I've heard people say they could pray in tongues so they believed they were baptized in the Holy Spirit, but at the same time they were not sure they really were.

Another way of losing your power is through overeating. I said earlier that your body is like a conductor. If you are overfed, the power will not flow as it ought to. It will be like a wire that is not pure enough to conduct electricity. If you eat three times a day, God cannot use you as He ought to. This is terribly bad news to some people. The Bible recommends a maximum of two meals per day. Recall the story of Elijah when God gave him a hideout by Brook Cherith, away from Jezebel's threats on his life. God sent birds to feed him twice a day. If God felt that Elijah needed to eat three times a day, He would have sent the birds three times. If you overeat, you will lose your power.

Too much comfort can also lead to loss of power. Most modern churches started off small, with great godly zeal, but when they became big and comfortable, they relaxed and their power decreased. My prayer is that God will never give me so much comfort that I will feel I do not need Him anymore.

Another way of losing your power is through believing strange doctrines.

> Then we will no longer be infants, tossed back and
> forth by the waves and blown here and there by every
> wind of teaching and by the cunning and craftiness of
> men in their deceitful scheming. (Ephesians 4:14)

The devil may use false teachings to rob you of your blessings. Run away from anything that is not completely based on the word of God, no matter how charismatic or convincing the teacher.

Flattery can also burst your power tank:

> Whoever flatters his neighbor is spreading a net for his
> feet. (Proverbs 29:5)

The person who flatters you is preparing you for destruction. You have to be very careful. We have an example in Judges:

> *So Delilah said to Samson, "Tell me the secret of your great strength and how you can be tied up and subdued."* (Judges 16:6)

Delilah called Samson a man of great strength, but by the time the story ended, great strength was a stranger to him.

So what must you do to regain the power? First, discover what went wrong and make amends. If you have been eating too much, you need to fast. If you have been listening to the wrong teachings, come back to the pure, undiluted word of God. If you doubted, come back to God and tell Him that you will believe Him all the way. If you find that you are too comfortable, spiritually or physically, then cut off all those things that make you so. For example, if you have the type of bed that seduces you to sleep and skip prayers, sleep on the floor. By the time you have done it for three days your power will return. Cut off those who have been flattering you, and deliberately refuse to be their friend anymore.

After reparation comes the return journey to the Lord.

> *I sought the Lord and he answered me, he delivered me from all my fears. Those who look to him are radiant, their faces are never covered with shame.*
>
> (Psalm 34:4-5)

When you go back to God, you must be prepared to stay with him until He is ready to answer you. You must remember that you are the one who lost something; if you want it back, you must wait until He gives it to you. God will give your power back to you if you are determined—but it may not be as easy as when you first got it.

Retention is Better Than Recovery

If God gives you power and you lose it, the time while it is lost will be the saddest period of your life. Those who have lost the power of the Holy Spirit will understand this statement better than anyone, but if you already have the power and you do not want to lose it, what should you do?

To keep your power, you must first remain in constant contact with its source: the Holy Spirit. Let us use an illustration. If you drop a heating element into a bucket of water, very soon the water will boil. While the water is boiling, it takes heat from the heating element. As long as it is connected to the power source, the water gets hotter. But when you remove it from the power source, it gets colder and colder and so does the water. Very soon, the heating element and the water are both cold. Therefore, if you are "hot" today with the Holy Spirit and you later lose contact with Him, very soon you will become cold. You must also remain in contact with children of God who are strong in the Lord.

The second thing you must do is to remain forever thirsty for the power of God. It is those who are thirsty that God will continue to pour water on.

> *For I will pour water on the thirsty land and streams on the dry ground; I will pour out my Spirit on your offspring and my blessings on your descendants.*
>
> (Isaiah 44:3)

If you have power and you keep asking for more, He will give you more but you must stay with Him. If you are thirsty, you look for water to drink. If you are not thirsty, then you do not need water. Be thirsty for the Holy Spirit.

Third, you must never forget the reason God gave you the power.

> *But you will receive power when the Holy Spirit comes on you and you will be my witnesses in Jerusalem and in all Judea and Samaria and to the ends of the earth.*
>
> (Acts 1: 8)

He gave us His power so that we can witness and win souls. If you get the power and you refuse to do so, you will lose it. The power of God is ours not for fun, nor to be hoarded. The more you witness, the more empowered you become.

You must also be moderate in everything you do.

> *Everyone who competes in the game goes into strict training. They do it to get a crown that will not last, but we do it to get a crown that will last forever. Therefore I do not run like a man running aimlessly, I do not fight like a man beating the air. No, I beat my body and make it my slave so that after I have preached to others, I myself will not be disqualified for the prize.* (1 Corinthians 9:25-27)

The Bible says we are allowed to covet spiritual gifts and powers. Therefore, you can always ask for more and God will always give it to you.

God once talked to me about something called flying time. Pilots are upgraded based on how long they have been flying, measured in hours. God asked, "If I wanted to employ a pilot, what will be my criteria? Would I employ a pilot who has flown for a thousand hours or the one who has flown for two thousand hours?" He told me that those who have won my respect because of the great power of God that they have, have "flown" longer than I have. I asked how they did so, and God led me to Isaiah:

> *But those who hope in the Lord will renew their strength. They will soar on wings like eagles; they will run and not grow weary, the will walk and not be faint.*
> (Isaiah 40:31)

Those who wait on the Lord and pray fervently in tongues are building up their flying time. God told me that although I had been praying, it had been for "bread and butter." Those who pray in tongues always pray for mysteries, the deep things of God.

god, the нoly spirit

There are people who have not flown for even one hour because they have not been baptized in the Holy Spirit and therefore they do not speak in tongues. There are also those who have been baptized in the Holy Spirit but who only pray in tongues occasionally.

I want to fly higher every day, but you cannot get off the ground if you are not born-again. If you are not born-again, how can you be baptized in the Holy Spirit? If you are born-again but not baptized in the Holy Spirit, tell Jesus today that you want to be baptized. And if you have been baptized in the Holy Spirit, why don't you increase your flying time?

chapter 6

purity and the gifts of the holy spirit

god requires purity before power

Our God is a holy God who demands that His children be like Him. There are several reasons for this. Those who possess the gifts of God are usually targets of attacks from the enemy. The gifts of God are precious and are meant for only the pure and holy. And the possessor of the gifts of God must not be a castaway in the end.

God demands purity before giving power:

> *Be perfect therefore as your heavenly Father is perfect.*
> (Matthew 5:48)

Those things that God will give are holy so those who will receive them must be holy.

The moment you begin to use the gifts of God, the enemy is bound to attack. For instance, when you put your gifts of healing into full gear, you can be sure that Satan, who put those you healed in the bondage of sickness, will be in hot pursuit of your life. You are engaging in a hot battle with Satan and if you are not holy, he will overcome you.

Therefore this is what the Lord says: "If you repent, I will restore you that you may serve me; if you utter worthy not worthless words, you will be my spokesman. Let this people turn to you but you must not turn to them. I will make you a wall to this people, a fortified wall of bronze; they will fight against you but will not overcome you, for I am with you to rescue and save you. I will save you from the hands of the wicked and redeem you from the grasp of the cruel.

(Jeremiah 15:19-21)

The prerequisite for all these promises is that you must return to God and separate the precious things from the vile things. In other words, you must be holy. Then you will be His mouthpiece and whatever you say will happen. When you begin to do this, the enemy will rise up against you but will not overcome you. Do not ask for the gifts of God if you do not want to live a holy life.

When you possess the gifts of God, you will become an instrument of honor for God's use. The basic qualifications for being an instrument of honor are listed in Timothy:

In a large house there are articles not only of gold and silver but also of wood and clay, some are for noble purposes and some are for ignoble. If a man cleanses himself from the latter, he would be an instrument for noble purposes, made holy; useful to the master and prepared to do any good work. (2 Timothy 2:20-21)

If you want to become an instrument of honor, you must purge yourself from all uncleanness. Once God gives you His gifts, wherever you go, people will recognize you as an instrument of the Almighty God. Therefore you have to be absolutely holy.

The gifts of God are very precious. They cannot be bought, but God wants everybody to have them. Poor people and rich people can have the gifts of God, but all must be holy.

Do not give dogs what is sacred; do not throw your
pearls to pigs. If you do, they may trample them under
their feet and then turn and tear you to pieces.

(Matthew 7:6)

As far as God is concerned, sinners are dogs, whether they are rich or poor. His children are called sons and daughters. If you are not born again, you are as a dog in God's eyes.

Another reason why we must be holy before we can receive the gifts of the Holy Spirit is to help us qualify for Heaven. Using the gifts of God to heal the sick, for example, is admirable but you must make sure you get to Heaven, too. The Bible tells us clearly that "without holiness no one will see the Lord." (Hebrews 12:14)

Basic Gifts Must Be Developed Before Receiving Other Gifts

Everyone on earth is given certain basic gifts or talents. God wants you to develop your basic talents before asking for more. Many of us who have these basic gifts may not want to develop them, but if you do not, you are not likely to get any more gifts. For example, there is a one called the gift of service, which involves ensuring that the Sanctuary is clean and beautiful. You do not have to pray to God to be able to perform these services. Nevertheless, some of us think that these are menial jobs and we are too important to do them. If you feel too big to do them, then you are too big for the gifts of the Holy Spirit.

In 1 Corinthians 16:15-16, we meet some people said to be addicted to the work of the saints. The Bible says they are superior Christians, the type to whom you must submit and give honor. Jesus Himself said that He had not come to be ministered to but to be a minister or servant to many. However, many of us do not want to serve yet we want the power of God. God will not give His powers to lazy people. This is because the moment He gives you power, things will begin to happen that you will not be able to handle unless you are ready and willing to serve.

Another basic quality that you must develop before God can give you the gifts of the Holy Spirit is the gift of giving. Some people are so miserly that it seems excruciatingly painful for them to give to others, but they always want to receive. Such people will not get anything from God because God gives His gifts so that you can pass them on to others. God has no use for stagnant waters but loves flowing rivers. The more you give others, the more God will give you.

You may say that you do not give because you are poor. In 2 Corinthians 8:1-5, we are told about a church in Macedonia that had the gift of giving, even though they were extremely poor. Some people do not even know how to give, and some prefer to give to their dogs rather than to human beings. Those who know how to give also know how to receive from God.

God wants you to be able to give. The moment you keep His gifts, He will stop giving to you. It is therefore important to learn how to give and to do so cheerfully because God loves a cheerful giver. (2 Corinthians 9:6-12) When you give, people will thank God because of you, and He will cause grace to flow to you so that you continue to have even more to give.

The gifts of god are in three categories

There are different kinds of spirits—lying spirits, seducing spirits, spirits of error and so on. There is only one spirit that is Holy, the Spirit of God. Any spirit that is not holy is not from God, so if you meet any prophet who prophesies but lives in sin, be sure that he is but a henchman for Satan. The Bible states that you must check every spirit against the word of God:

> *Dear Friends, do not believe every spirit but test the spirits to see whether they are from God, because many false prophets have gone out into the world. This is how you can recognize the Spirit of God; Every spirit that acknowledges that Jesus Christ has come in the flesh is from God. But every spirit that does not acknowledge Jesus is not from God. This is the spirit of the*

antichrist, which you have heard is coming and even now is already in the world. (1 John 4:1-3)

There are nine main gifts of the Holy Spirit:

Now to each one the manifestation of the Spirit is given for the common good. To one there is given through the Spirit the message of wisdom, to another the message of knowledge by the same Spirit. To another faith by the same Spirit, to another gifts of healing by that one Spirit, to another miraculous powers, to another prophesy, to another distinguishing between spirits, to another speaking in different kinds of tongues.
(1 Corinthians 12:7- 10)

These gifts can be classified into three groups:

Revelation gifts

- The word of wisdom
- The word of knowledge
- The discerning of spirits

Inspiration gifts

- Prophesy
- Diverse kinds of tongues
- Interpretation of tongues

Power gifts

- Faith
- Healing
- Working of miracles

chapter 7

the gift of
the word of wisdom

The gift of the *word* of wisdom is different from the gift of wisdom. Before we can say much about the word of wisdom, we have to know the meaning of wisdom itself: the use of knowledge for one's benefit. For example, if you are driving along a road and a sign warns you of a narrow bridge ahead, if you are a wise driver, you will ease up on the gas pedal. The knowledge is the road sign; you apply wisdom by slowing down.

If you are told that fire burns yet you put your hand in it and get burned, you are not wise but foolish. When the government says that if you are caught with hard drugs you will be jailed, if you are a wise person, you will not touch them at all. The Bible states that the soul that sins will die. (Ezekiel 18:4) If you are a wise person, you will run away from sin and apply the Bible's teachings to live a holy life because no sinner will see God. The Bible tells us that wisdom is very important:

> *Wisdom is supreme; therefore get wisdom. Though it cost all you have, get understanding.* (Proverbs 4:7)

In other words, God is saying that whatever else you want to get from Him, you must make sure that you get wisdom first. If you are wise, you will not use God's gifts to hurt yourself.

There are three major types of wisdom: the wisdom of Satan, the wisdom of man and the wisdom of God. Satanic wisdom is corrupted wisdom, human wisdom is at times called common sense, and divine wisdom is pure and excellent.

> *But if you harbor bitter envy and selfish ambition in your hearts, do not boast about it or deny the truth. Such wisdom does not come down from heaven but it is earthly, unspiritual of the devil. For where you have envy and selfish ambition, there you find disorder and every evil practice.* (James 3:14-16)

It is the wisdom of Satan that makes people stab others in the back for gain. It makes people flock to secret societies and the occult. Those who fall prey are told that they will enjoy promotions and favor from high quarters. It sustains sorcery, it destroys, and it gives riches through evil means. The wisdom of Satan is contrary to the will of God and is rooted in hypocrisy.

There is also the wisdom of man, sometimes referred to as common sense. This is the type of wisdom you use when budgeting, if you want to build a house or when a nation wants to go to war. Jesus said:

> *Suppose one of you wants to build a tower. Will he not first sit down and estimate the cost to see if he has enough money to complete it? For if he lays the foundation and is not able to finish it, everyone who sees it will ridicule him, saying, "This fellow began to build and was not able to finish." Or suppose a king is about to go to war against another king. Will he not first sit down and consider whether he is able with ten thousand men to oppose the one coming against him with twenty thousand? If he is not able, he will send a delegation while the other is still a long way off and will ask for terms of peace.* (Luke 14:28-32)

The wisdom of man also includes the "wisdom" of bribing law enforcement agents or other officials. Some people wrongly interpret what Jesus said about giving unto Caesar what belongs to Caesar and to God what belongs to God. (Matthew 22:21) What Jesus meant when He used this phrase was that we should pay our taxes.

The wisdom of man also inspires lying for business gain, and it tries to present charms, the occult and sorcery as acceptable activities because the tokens used are all found on God's earth. This is contrary to the will of God even though it looks sensible. Common sense does not work with God because, according to the Bible, the just shall live by faith (Habakkuk 2:4). If you want to live by common sense, God will fold His arms and allow you to do your own thing—without Him.

The wisdom of man can cause you to prosper, but only in this world. It cannot take you to the Kingdom of God.

> *I thought to myself. "Look I have grown and increased in wisdom more than anyone who has ruled over Jerusalem before me; I have experienced much of wisdom and knowledge. Then I applied myself to the understanding of wisdom and also of madness and folly but I learned that this too is a chasing after the wind. For with much wisdom comes much sorrow; the more knowledge the more grief."* (Ecclesiastes 1:16-18)

Having knowledge is good, but you must not be deceived into thinking that you know better than God. Such knowledge results in futility. The Bible tells us that the greatest wisdom among men has no place with God:

> *For the foolishness of God is wiser than man's wisdom and the weakness of God is stronger than man's strength.* (1 Corinthians 1:25)

You cannot use common sense to understand or interpret Christianity. All the stories that relate to Jesus Christ cannot be understood by common sense alone. That a virgin conceives does not have a place in modern science. That angels warned Joseph to run away from King Herod instead of protecting him and the Child has no place in common sense. That the miracle-working Jesus could not save Himself from His detractors does not make human sense. The same goes for his death and resurrection. If He knew that He would resurrect, why did He have to die? However, whether it makes sense or not, Jesus' resurrection brought salvation and healing. It brought deliverance, miracles, signs and wonders, and peace. The greatest and best type of wisdom is the wisdom of God.

> But the wisdom that comes from heaven is first of all pure; then peace-loving, considerate, submissive, full of mercy and good fruit, impartial and sincere.
> (James 3:17)

God's wisdom is holy. It is neither the wisdom of hypocrisy nor that which you use for character assassination. The wisdom of God shows you how to reach Heaven, gives you sober reflections on salvation, and helps you understand that all the commandments of God are for our benefit. It makes you think about Heaven and the things of God. The wisdom of God allows you to move closer to Him and do His will.

Divine wisdom is not limited to spiritual matters only. We can obtain divine wisdom for our business, for leadership, and for everyday living. We need to note that God knows the past, present and future. He has an infinite storehouse of information, but gives only a bit at the right time.

> There are different kinds of gifts but the same Spirit. There are different kinds of service but the same Lord. There are different kinds of working but the same God works all of them in all men. Now to each one the manifestation of the Spirit is given for the common good. To one there is given through the Spirit the message of

wisdom, to another the message of knowledge by the same Spirit. (1 Corinthians 12:4-8)

For what do we need the word of wisdom? It can be obtained from God for several purposes. For example, if you are a clothing manufacturer with divine wisdom, you will discover that you prosper above all your competitors. God guides you supernaturally in your profession. If you are a furniture maker and you have this gift, you will suddenly find your factory producing exquisite furniture. In other words, you can get this divine wisdom for your day-to-day business transactions. You can ask for the wisdom of God for success.

> *Then the Lord said to Moses, "See I have chosen Bezaleel son of Uri, the son of Hur, of the tribe of Judah and I have filled him with the Spirit of God, with skill, ability and knowledge in all kinds of crafts—to make artistic designs for work in gold, silver and bronze, to cut and set stones, to work in wood and to engage in all kinds of craftsmanship."* (Exodus 31:1-5)

Whatever your role as a leader may be, whether you are a manager, a supervisor or a pastor, you need supernatural wisdom. We can ask for the privilege of being a good leader, for without the wisdom of God no leader can be successful.

> *Now Joshua son of Nun was filled with the spirit of wisdom because Moses had laid his hands on him. So the Israelites listened to him and did what the Lord had commanded Moses.* (Deuteronomy 34:9)

Joshua was full of the spirit of wisdom and he was successful in reaching the Promised Land, but you need this wisdom even if you are not a leader.

> *Trust in the Lord with all your heart and lean not on your own understanding; in all your ways acknowledge*

him and he will make your paths straight. Do not be wise in your own eyes; fear the Lord and shun evil.

(Proverbs 3:5-7)

If you will allow God to direct you in all your paths, He will do so. Those who are directed by God will never go astray. Many people have made mistakes they could have avoided if only they had the wisdom of God.

Above all, if you really want to understand spiritual things, you need this wisdom from above.

We have not received the Spirit of the world but the Spirit who is from God that we may understand what God has freely given us. This is what we speak not in words taught us by the Spirit, expressing spiritual truths in spiritual words. The man without the Spirit does not accept the things that come from the Spirit of God for they are foolishness to him and he cannot understand them because they are spiritually discerned. (1 Corinthians 2:12-14)

Many of us have found it difficult to explain what we mean by being born-again. People ask whether it means baptism, or fellowship, or confirmation. When you become born-again you will know, and you will not understand spiritual things until you do.

How can you explain to a doctor that to cure a stomach ulcer, all you need do is pray? He will laugh at you. He just cannot understand, even though he is a wise person by the standards of the world. We understand because God has given us His wisdom, which we need more than any other gift because wisdom is stronger than power. If you have His wisdom, it will not be long before you have His power, because He will show you how to get everything you want.

A word aptly spoken is like apples of gold in settings of silver. (Proverbs 25:11)

purpose for which this gift is given

There are several reasons why God may give you the gift of the word of wisdom. God never wants problems to persist in His children's lives, particularly those that are leaders of men. There will be times when you will be faced with many difficult situations because the devil wants to ridicule or confuse you. A man of God can find himself in a tight corner, but with the gift of the word of wisdom, he can maneuver out of the traps of Satan.

A very good case in point was Solomon's judgment on a maternity suit brought by two women. Bible history tell us that when Solomon became king, he was very young. He recognized that he had no knowledge in governance, so when God gave him the opportunity he asked for wisdom. Thus when he was faced with two women and a dead child he simply used the wisdom God gave him.

> *Then the King said, "Bring me a sword." So they brought a sword for the King. He then gave an order: "Cut the living child in two and give half to one and half to the other." The woman whose son was alive was filled with compassion for her son and said to the king. "Please, my Lord, give her the living baby! Don't kill him!" But the other said, "Neither I nor you shall have him: Cut him in two!" Then the King gave his ruling: "Give the living baby to the first woman. Do not kill him; she is his mother."* (1 Kings 3:24-27)

No human being could have given that judgment. It was God who spoke through Solomon.

God often provides the word of wisdom to confuse the enemy. The greatest battle that we fight really has to do with what we say. The devil knows that whatever we say is written in Heaven and we must give account of it on the last day. Therefore, the devil constantly brings all types of questions to us through people. For example, someone asked a child of God what he would do if his father sent him to buy cigarettes. The word of wisdom came to the child of God and in response he asked the fellow what he would do if his father was drunk and he asked him to bring a loaded gun with which he had tried to kill himself before.

The word of wisdom can be used when a child of God encounters challenges from the opposition and it seems the enemy is about to prevail. We have an example in the Bible when some people asked Jesus whether it was lawful to pay tax. They knew quite well that Caesar reigned over the Jews at this time and Jews were not happy with this situation, and they also knew that the Jews had to pay taxes to Caesar. If Jesus had said it was lawful to pay tax to Caesar, they would have told the other Jews that Jesus was against them. If He said it was unlawful to pay tax to Caesar, they would have accused Him of breaking the law. Whatever answer He gave would have caught Him in a trap. Matthew 22:17-22 tells us the full story. The saying, "Give to Caesar what belongs to Caesar," had a lot of meaning then. At that time, the Hebrews always sent curses to Caesar. When Jesus replied the Pharisees, He was not just talking about taxes. All who heard him were surprised. They tried to set Him up, but He had the wisdom of God. He did not come to abolish the rule of law but to fulfill it.

In another plot, some people brought a woman who was caught in the act of adultery to Jesus and said that the law stipulated that she had to be stoned to death. (John 8:3-8) They asked Him what to do about the matter, since He did not come to destroy but to save. If He had agreed that the woman should be killed they would question His claim of being the Savior. If He said they should allow her to go free, they would convict Him of breaking the law. As this was going on, God gave Jesus a word of wisdom. Jesus told them that He was not saying that they should not stone her; after all, that was what the law said. However, anyone who had never sinned himself should be the first person to cast the first stone. They found themselves caught in the trap they tried to set for Jesus Christ.

These are beautiful examples of how God can use the word of wisdom to confuse the enemy. Here is another:

> *Jesus entered the Temple courts and while he was teaching, the chief priests and the elders of the people came to him. "By what authority are you doing these things?" they asked. "And who gave you this authority?" Jesus replied, "I will also ask you one question. If you answer me, I will tell you by what authority I am doing these things. John's baptism – where did it come from? Was it from heaven or from men?" They discussed it among themselves and said, "If we say, "From heaven," he will ask, "Then why didn't you believe him? But if we say, "From men," we are afraid of the people, for they all hold that John was a prophet." So they answered Jesus, "We don't know." Then he said, "Neither will I tell you by what authority I am doing these things."* (Matthew 21:23-27)

If Jesus had said He was using the authority of God, they would have called Him a liar since He was not a high priest. If He had said He was using His own authority, they would have debunked this too. He was aware of their trap so He asked them about John the Baptist and his authority. Thus they found themselves caught in their own trap.

The word of wisdom can put your enemy to shame and give glory to God. Just a sentence or a word can deliver a child of God from trouble and bring deliverance.

> *The commander ordered Paul to be taken into the barracks. He directed that he be flogged and questioned in order to find out why the people were shouting at him like this. As they stretched him out to flog him, Paul said to the centurion standing there, "Is it legal for you to flog a Roman citizen who hasn't even been found guilty?" When the Centurion heard this he went to the*

commander and reported it. "What are you going to do?" he asked. "This man is a Roman citizen." Then the commander went to Paul and asked, "Tell me, are you a Roman citizen?" "Yes, I am," he answered. Then the commander said, "I had to pay a big price for my citizenship." "But I was born a citizen," Paul replied. Those who were about to question him withdrew immediately. The commander himself was alarmed when he realized that he had put Paul, a Roman citizen in chains. (Acts 22:24-29)

Paul's detractors wanted to scourge him but God delivered him with just one question. The word of wisdom is usually brief but it does marvelous things.

God also uses the word of wisdom to transform a fool into a wise person, allowing the fool to defeat the wise. In Acts 6:8-10, the Bible tells us about Stephen. When the Deacons were elected Stephen was among them, not because he was educated but because he was filled with the Spirit of God. Whoever is filled with the Spirit of God certainly will have the gifts of God, including wisdom. Among the detractors of Stephen was Saul of Tarsus who was very educated.

God also gives the word of wisdom for direction. We have an example in the case of Paul when he was pondering where to go and preach. In his dream, he was told to go to Macedonia. Many times we ask for direction from God and, at such times, He will send the word of wisdom to us.

The best example of how God uses the word of wisdom to set His people free and to elevate them is found in Daniel 2 in the story of King Nebuchadnezzar and his dream. The king had forgotten his dream and decreed that all the wise men in the city should be killed if they could not remind him of the dream and interpret it. Daniel went to God and asked Him for the dream and its interpretation. In Daniel's sleep, God told him. Can you imagine the indescribable joy that filled Daniel's heart the morning after?

How the Gift Manifests

This can happen in several ways. It could come in the form of an audible voice; that is, God can speak to you directly. God also gives the word of wisdom through dreams and visions as we saw earlier.

> *During the night the mystery was revealed to Daniel in a vision. Then Daniel praised the God of heaven and said: Praise be to the name of God forever and ever; wisdom and power are his. He changes times and seasons; sets up kings and deposes them. He gives wisdom to the wise and knowledge to the discerning. He reveals deep and hidden things; he knows what lies in darkness and light dwells with him. I thank and praise you, O God of my fathers; You have given me wisdom and power you have made known to me what we asked of you, you have made known to us the dream of the king.*
> (Daniel 2:19-23)

If you have the gift of the word of wisdom and you have a problem that is too big for you to solve, you need never worry again.

The gift can come by way of prophecy, and also through the Bible as you read it:

> *Your word is a lamp to my feet, and a light to my path.*
> (Psalm 119:105)

God used the Bible method to help me when I was preparing my Ph.D. thesis. I was reading the encounter of the Israelites at the Red Sea and how it was parted for them to cross on dry ground. Immediately the word of wisdom whizzed through my mind, showing me how I could use the theory of the parted sea to solve a mathematical problem that I wanted solved.

You need the gift of the word of wisdom even though it can be very delicate and subtle. When it begins to operate in your life, God starts you off with commands that may seem uncomfortable, but if you obey Him, your obedience will be rewarded.

How to get the gift of wisdom

You have to ask for the gift of the word of wisdom. If you want this gift and you have been saved and sanctified, just ask God. He will give it to you. However, if you are yet to be saved and you ask for this gift, you will not get it.

chapter 8

The gift of
the word of knowledge

*To one there is given through the Spirit the message of
wisdom, to another the message of knowledge by the
same Spirit.* (1 Corinthians 12:8)

The word of knowledge is
a fragment of god's knowledge

God has an inexhaustible reservoir of knowledge. He knows everything that has ever happened and everything yet to happen. God
knows everything concerning you; a strand of your hair cannot fall
down without God's knowledge. Thus Jesus Christ already knows
what your challenges are.

*Praise be to the name of God forever and ever; wisdom
and power are his. He changes times and seasons; sets
up kings and deposes them. He gives wisdom to the
wise and knowledge to the discerning. He reveals deep
and hidden things; he knows what lies in darkness and
light dwells with him.* (Daniel 2:20-22)

God knows everything that is hidden. From time to time, He shows you a little bit of it, if you are His. Then people will remark about your knowledge. But you cannot compel Him to give; He is the One who decides.

> *Do not keep talking so proudly or let your mouth speak such arrogance, for the Lord is a God who knows and by him deeds are weighed.* (1 Samuel 2:3)

If you think you have knowledge, you had better be careful so you don't become proud. God knows the intrinsic value of your words, thoughts and deeds, and can withdraw all the knowledge you arrogantly lay claim to. As for Him, there is no limit to His knowledge, while we are very limited indeed. We even recognize how limited our knowledge is by issuing certificates and diplomas qualifying what we have but we cannot measure the knowledge of God.

> *Do you not know? Have you not heard? The Lord is the everlasting God, the Creator of the ends of the Earth. He will not grow tired or weary and his understanding no one can fathom.* (Isaiah 40:28)

God knows all our needs:

> *Do not be like them for your Father knows what you need before you ask Him.* (Matthew 6:8)

Many times we doubt that God know enough. However, He knows everything, including our thoughts:

> *And again, The Lord knows that the thoughts of the wise, are futile.* (1 Corinthians 3:20)

From time to time, God reveals a little bit of what He knows to us. He could do this through an audible voice or show it in a vision, or it could take the form of other spiritual revelations.

god's purpose for the word of knowledge

God gives the word of knowledge to His people when He wants to execute judgment. For instance, when God wanted to destroy Sodom and Gomorrah, He revealed His plans to Abraham:

> Then the Lord said, "Shall I hide from Abraham what I am about to do? Abraham will surely become a great and powerful nation and all nations on earth will be blessed through him. For I have chosen him so that he will direct all his children and his household after him to keep the way of the Lord by doing what is right and just, so that the Lord will bring about for Abraham what he has promised him." Then the Lord said, "The outcry against Sodom and Gomorrah is so great and their sin so grievous that I will go down and see if what they have done is as bad as the outcry that has reached me. If not, I will know." (Genesis 18:17-21)

God knew that the people of Sodom and Gomorrah were perverse. He informed Abraham so he could plead for them. In this case the word of knowledge was given audibly, as it also was when God wanted to destroy the family of Eli, the priest.

> And the Lord said to Samuel, "See I am about to do something in Israel that will make the ears of everyone who hears of it tingle. At that time I will carry out against Eli everything I spoke against his family from beginning to end. For I told him that I would judge his family forever because of the sin he knew about; his sons made themselves contemptible and he failed to restrain them. Therefore, I swore to the house of Eli, '"The guilt of Eli's house will never be atoned for by sacrifice or offering.'"" (1 Samuel 3:11-14)

The Lord also used the word of knowledge to reveal the secret of sin or the sinful intentions of Ananias and Sapphira in Acts 5:1-5.

How did Peter know their plans? The Holy Spirit revealed the secret to him. It is a very dangerous thing to lie to a man of God. The result is almost without doubt—death unless you confess quickly and repent. When you do something secretly in your room and you think God does not see you, you are mistaken. God knows your thoughts as well as your deeds. If you are a deceitful person and you do not want to be exposed, you had better avoid those filled with the Holy Spirit. Recall that Gehazi's greed got him leprosy for life:

> Then he went in and stood before his master Elisha. "Where have you been, Gehazi?" Elisha asked. "Your servant didn't go anywhere," Gehazi answered. But Elisha said to him, "Was not my spirit with you when the man got down from his chariot to meet you? Is this the time to take money or to accept clothes, olive groves, vineyards, flocks, herds or menservants and maidservants?" (2 Kings 5:25-26)

God revealed to Elisha how Gehazi secretly met Naaman and received gratification, and revealed to Elisha why Gehazi wanted it. Our God is to be highly revered and we must also respect His true servants. Through the word of knowledge, God can reveal your enemy to you. However, He may prevent you from making the knowledge public.

The Lord uses the word of knowledge to guide His own so that they will not make mistakes. Often all we can see is the surface while God has deep insights. We have an illustration in 1 Samuel 16:6-12 when God sent Samuel to anoint King Saul's successor in Jesse's house. When Samuel saw Eliab, Jesse's first son, Samuel was carried away by Eliab's stature and charisma. God told him that Eliab's heart was not worthy. Many things happen that we do not understand because we merely look at outward appearances, but God looks at the heart.

In many churches, a pastor is chosen because the fellow can preach well, looks rich or has a degree. Problems that manifest soon after the choice is made can confirm how wrong the choice was. If you choose under the direction of God, you will be amazed by how many popular candidates according to human wisdom are God's rejects. When you ask God to choose for you, especially if you are looking for a future partner, God's choice may not appeal to you at all. However, do not worry because if the choice is made by God, you will be happy for the rest of your life. If you choose for yourself, there will be repercussions.

God also uses the word of knowledge to warn about impending dangers. One example is in Kings when the king of Israel and the Syrian king were at war.

> *Now the King of Syria was at war with Israel. After conferring with his officers, he said, "I will set up my camp in such and such a place." The man of God sent word to the king of Israel: "Beware of passing that place, because the Syrians are going down there."*

> *So the king of Israel checked on the place indicated by the man of God. Time and again Elisha warned the king, so that he was on his guard in such places. This enraged the king of Syria. He summoned his officers and demanded of them, "Will you not tell me which of us is on the side of the king of Israel?" "None of us, my lord the king," said one of his officers, "But Elisha, the prophet who is in Israel, tells the king of Israel the very words you speak in your bedroom." (2 Kings 6:8-12)*

Elisha was filled with the Holy Spirit. God revealed all the plans of the king of Syria to him and Elisha told the king of Israel. This is the word of knowledge. God can use it to inform you about family matters, irrespective of the physical distance between you and your family, and He will tell you what to do.

Our second example is Paul's trip to Rome in Acts 27:9-10. Paul had warned that the journey would be a dangerous one but the others did not believe him. The captain of the ship said that there would be no problem, but the journey was nearly a tragedy. When a true prophet of God predicts or prophesies, believe him because it will happen.

God also uses the word of knowledge as a map or a guide for a journey. In Acts 10:1-10, all the information needed for the journey was given to Cornelius, to the last detail. When God directs you like this, you cannot make a mistake. He will never let you go astray. Another example is in Acts where a definite description was given to Ananias:

> *In Damascus, there was a disciple named Ananias. The Lord called to him in a vision, "Ananias!" "Yes, Lord" he answered. The Lord told him, "Go to the house of Judas on Straight Street and ask for a man from Tarsus named Saul for he is praying. In a vision he has seen a man named Ananias come and place his hands on him to restore his sight."* (Acts 9:10-12)

This is the word of knowledge at its best. God also uses it to encourage His servants and to give them prior knowledge of miracles about to happen. There came a time in 1 Kings 19:9-18 when Elijah became discouraged. He thought that he was the only surviving prophet of God, but God told him that there were seven thousand still under God's divine protection. Here he used the word of knowledge to provide comfort and encouragement. And when Elijah was on Mount Carmel in 1 Kings 18-41, God revealed to him that it would rain even when there was no cloud yet in the sky. At the peak of famine, God told him that there would be more than enough food to eat within twenty-four hours.

God uses the word of knowledge to herald His signs and wonders. Once during a crusade, God revealed to us that there was a woman in the congregation whose marriage was on the verge of collapse and that if the woman could come out, her marriage would be saved. We told the congregation and to our surprise, a woman spoke up and said her husband had already filed a divorce suit against her. We told her that by the time she arrived home, the situation would have changed and that the husband would have turned a new leaf. She came back later to give her testimony that what we said came to pass.

At the same gathering, God revealed to us that there was a man who had contacted a disease from sleeping around. I did not ask the person involved to come out publicly but to meet us after the meeting. He came and we prayed for him and, two weeks later, he gave his testimony.

God uses the word of knowledge to deliver His people and make them victorious. Once God told us that there was a woman in one of our crusades who could not conceive because something had blocked her womb. God told us when the problem started. This woman came to the altar and we prayed for her. She gave the testimony that as we laid hands on her something like a ball fell from her abdomen.

How to obtain the gift

The gift of the word of knowledge is not as freely given as the word of wisdom. Only those who are in a covenant relationship with God can get it, those who have given their all to God.

> *For I have chosen him so that he will direct all his children and his household after him to keep the way of the Lord by doing what is right and just, so that the Lord will bring about for Abraham what he has promised him.* (Genesis 18:19)

God could not help but tell Abraham what He wanted to do because He had already made a covenant with him. Paul gave all to Christ that He might know Him. Cornelius also gave his all to God as we read in Acts:

> *At Caesarea there was a man named Cornelius, a centurion in what was known as the Italian Regiment. He and all his family were devout and God-fearing; he*

gave generously to those in need and prayed to God regularly. (Acts 10:1-2)

Jesus Christ said:

You are my friends if you do what I command. I no longer call you servants, because a servant does not know his master's business. Instead I have called you friends for everything that I learned from my Father I have made known to you. You did not choose me but I chose you and appointed you to go and bear fruit – fruit that will last. Then the Father will give you whatever you ask in my name. (John 15:14-16)

Anyone who is not ready to surrender all cannot obtain this gift. If Jesus Christ cannot say of you that you are His friend and that whatever He wants you to do you will do, He will not give it to you. Those to whom God has given the gift of the word of knowledge are those who have determined that, in life and in death, they would serve the Lord. Do you want this gift? Are you ready to do the will of God wholeheartedly? It is only for children of God, so if you are not yet born-again, accept the Lord now. If you are already born-again, before you ask for this gift, tell Jesus that you surrender all.

chapter 9

The Gift of the Discerning of spirits

To another miraculous powers, to another prophesy, to another distinguishing between spirits, to another speaking in different kinds of tongues.

(1 Corinthians 12:10)

Differentiating Between Good and Evil

There are different kinds of spirits. Let us identify some of them from the Bible.

He called his twelve disciples to him and gave them authority to drive out evil spirits and to heal every disease and sickness. (Matthew 10:1)

Here the Bible mentions a type of spirit called evil or unclean. Another type is found in Timothy:

The Spirit clearly says that in later times some will abandon the faith and follow deceiving spirits and things taught by demons. (1 Timothy 4:1)

59

This text refers to deceiving or seducing spirits. In Kings we meet lying spirits:

> So now the Lord has put a lying spirit in the mouths of these prophets of yours. The Lord has decreed disaster for you. (1 Kings 22:23)

Some other types of spirits are described in John:

> We are from God and whoever knows God listens to us; but whoever is not from God does not listen to us. This is how we recognize the spirit of truth and the spirit of falsehood. (1 John 4:6)

These are the spirits of truth and the spirits of error. In John we also read about the spirit of the anti-Christ:

> But every spirit that does not acknowledge that Jesus is from God. This is the Spirit of the Anti-Christ which you have heard is coming and even now is already in the world. (1 John 4:3)

God made a place for the gift of the discerning of spirits because there are different types. We must able to identify what particular spirit is working at any particular time. For example, seducing spirits pretend they are good spirits. But if you have the gift of the discerning of spirits within you, no evil spirit can deceive you.

> Once when we were going to the place of prayer, we were met by a slave girl who had a spirit by which she predicted the future. She earned a great deal of money for her owners by fortune telling. This girl followed Paul and the rest of us; shouting, "These men are servants of the Most High God, who are telling you the way to be saved." She kept this up for many days. Finally Paul became so troubled that he turned around and said to the spirit, "In the name of Jesus Christ I

command you to come out of her!" At that moment the
spirit left her. (Acts 16:16-18)

The spirit displayed by the slave girl is called the spirit of divination, used by witch doctors, tarot card readers, astrologers and
psychics. She belonged to Satan, yet she recognized the children
of God. Many people preach the Gospel of Jesus Christ but the
spirit in them is not His. Wonders happen in many ministries and
people claim it is through the Name of Jesus Christ but they are
filled with evil spirits, especially the spirit of divination. How then
do we know the difference? If you have the gift of the discerning of
spirits, you will know the difference by seeing into the spiritual
realm.

Angels are spirits, but you cannot see them unless you have the
gift of the discerning of spirits. When your spiritual eyes are
opened, you will be able to see evil spirits and angels, both bad and
good. The job of a minister of God becomes easy with the gift of
seeing into the spiritual realm.

There are two types of worlds, the physical and the spiritual. Man
was created as a trinity: body, soul and spirit. We have two types of
eyes and two types of ears: physical and spiritual. The sinner's spiritual eyes are blind, but if you are a Christian filled with the Holy
Spirit, you can ask God to open your spiritual eyes to see spiritual
things. God may deliberately show you an angel or two, as it happened in the case of Samson's parents, or as it was with Gideon.
Mary, the mother of Jesus Christ, saw the angel and heard what he
had to say in Luke 1:26-28. When you have the gift of the discerning of spirits, not only will you be able to see them, you will also
be able to hear what they are saying and can talk with them if you
want.

why does god give the gift of the discerning of spirits?

When God wants to bring down judgment and sees a righteous
person among those to be destroyed, He will show that person

what is ahead. For example, in Genesis 18:17-22, God revealed to Abraham what He wanted to do with Sodom and Gomorrah. As terrible as the cities were, God really did not want to destroy them. He wanted to rescue the people so He sent angels to someone who could plead for them. God waited patiently for Abraham to do so. If Abraham had pleaded more persistently, perhaps the cities would have been saved.

Secondly, when something great and important is about to happen, or has happened, God gives this gift of the discerning of spirits to His beloved so they get to share in the full knowledge of His spiritual agenda. God revealed to Zacharias in Luke 1:11-17 that he would have a son. God opened his spiritual eyes to see the angel that brought the message. In Luke 1:26-37, God opened the spiritual eyes of Mary to see the angel that came to tell her that she would conceive. When God wanted to disclose to John the revelation about the last days, He opened his spiritual eyes to see those things that will come to pass:

> On the Lord's day I was in the Spirit and I heard behind me a loud voice like a trumpet, which said "Write a scroll what you see and send it to the seven churches; to Ephesus, Smyrna, Pergamum, Thyatira, Sardis, Philadelphia and Loadecia." I turned around to see the voice that was speaking to me. And when I turned I saw seven golden lampstands. (Revelation 1:10-12)

Thirdly, when God sees someone that must help Him perform a certain duty, He will open the spiritual eyes of that person and send an angel to him or her so He can explain clearly. For example, if God wants to deal with secret societies or the occult, He will open your eyes to see any defenses they may want to put in place. He would show you any scheme designed to hurt you and will open your eyes to see whatever danger lies ahead.

As God commissioned Gideon to save Israel, He sent an angel to talk to him. Gideon became bold enough to destroy the temple of his father's god. When God was about to send Moses to lead the

Israelites out of Egypt, He opened Moses' eyes to see things from the spiritual realm. It was with spiritual eyes that Moses saw the fire that did not consume the bush. (Exodus 3:2)

When Joshua was by the walls of Jericho, God opened his spiritual eyes and gave him the war plans. Joshua saw the angel that brought them. (Joshua 5:13) If it had been a human being that brought this message, he would not have believed. In Judges 13:3-5 God opened the eyes of a certain woman (who eventually became Samson's mother) to see spiritual things. Her son was not to drink alcohol because he would be specially dedicated to God's purpose.

God also opens spiritual eyes when one is in great danger, especially when all hope seems lost. Once you stand for God, He will help you to see hope for the future and how to overcome the dangers ahead. He will open your eyes to see that He is with you.

> Then he sent horses and chariots and a strong force there. They went by night and surrounded the city. When the servant of the man of God got up and went out early the next morning, an army with horses and chariots had surrounded the city. "Oh my lord, what shall we do?" the servant asked. "Don't be afraid," the prophet answered. "Those who are with us are more than those who are with them." And Elisha prayed, "O LORD, open his eyes so he may see." Then the Lord opened the servant's eyes and he looked and saw the hills full of horses and chariots of fire all around Elisha. (2 Kings 6:14-17)

Elisha saw the hosts of Heaven that surrounded him and his servant, but the servant could not see them. Very often, you may find your leader doing strange things that you may not understand. If you do not understand what he is doing, instead of arguing with him, ask God to open your eyes to share your leader's insights into the realm of the spirit.

Paul was confronted by a stormy sea-trip in Acts 27:23-24. All who were with him on the ship had lost hope of survival. In the night, the angel of the Lord came to assure Paul that they would make it to land.

When God wants to commend you as His beloved, He opens your spiritual eyes and comes to you Himself. That happened to Shadrach, Meshach and Abednego in the fiery furnace. It was God who joined them there to protect them and commend them for not bowing to idols. In Acts, when Stephen was being stoned, God opened the windows of Heaven so he could see the glory of God:

> But Stephen full of the Holy Spirit looked up to heaven and saw the glory of God and Jesus standing at the right hand of God. "Look" he said, "I see heaven open and the Son of Man standing at the right hand of God."
> (Acts 7:55-56)

When a Christian warrior has been fighting a battle and it appears he's becoming tired, God uses this medium to let him know that the glory waiting ahead is greater than all the suffering.

> I know a man in Christ who fourteen years ago was caught up to the third heaven. Whether it was in the body or out of the body, I do not know—God knows. And I know that this man—whether in the body or apart from the body I do not know, but God knows—was caught up to paradise. He heard inexpressible things, things that man is not permitted to tell.
> (2 Corinthians 12:2-4)

Paul had gone through much persecution and, when he was beginning to feel discouraged, God took him to the third heavens and showed him the glory awaiting him. There is also the case of Cornelius, to whom God sent an angel to deliver a special message. Remember that when God wanted to send Isaiah on a special assignment, he allowed him to see the glory of God. If God can show you where you are going, you do not need anyone preaching to you anymore. May God open your eyes.

How do we know when spirits are near and how do we identify them?

A spirit glided past my face and the hair on my body stood on end. It stopped but I could not tell what it was. A form stood before my eyes and I heard a hushed voice; Can a mortal be more righteous than God? Can a man be more pure than his Maker? (Job 4:15-17)

In this passage, the Bible tells us in clear terms that when a spirit is passing by, your hair stirs or you get goosebumps. If your hair goes back to normal immediately, discount it. Quickly say that you are covered by the Blood of Jesus Christ. If your hair remains standing, it means that the spirit has come to pay you a visit, for good or bad. At this stage, if you are already filled with the Holy Spirit, command the spirit to manifest itself in the mighty name of Jesus Christ. When the spirits or angels hear the His name, they have to obey. And when they manifest, do not run away. Find out whether the spirit is from God or the devil. The Bible gives us some instructions on how to do so:

But every spirit that does not acknowledge that Jesus, is from God. This is the Spirit of the Anti-Christ which you have heard is coming and even now is already in the world. (1 John 4:3)

To identify whether a spirit is good or evil, you can ask it if Jesus Christ has come in the flesh. If the spirit says no, then it is from the devil. If the answer is positive, then the spirit is from God.

Therefore I tell you that no one who is speaking by the Spirit of God says, "Jesus be cursed," and no one can say "Jesus is Lord" except by the Holy Spirit.
(1 Corinthians 12:3)

Ask whether Jesus Christ is forever blessed and if Jesus Christ is Lord. If both answers are positive, then you are talking with an angel. There is another test in Luke:

> *Then an angel of the Lord appeared to him, standing at the right side of the altar of incense. When Zechariah saw him he was startled and was gripped with fear. But the angel said to him: "Don't be afraid, Zechariah, your prayer has been heard. Your wife Elizabeth will bear you a son and you are to give him the name John."*
>
> (Luke 1:11-13)

Spirits from God will always say, "Fear not" to subdue your fears whereas evil spirits enjoy making you terrified. Any spirit that fails these tests, no matter how beautiful, is not from the Lord. Remember that the devil himself can appear as an angel of light.

Do you really want the important gift of the discerning of spirits? It is a terrible thing to go through life blindfolded, but God is willing to open your eyes if you are ready for it.

chapter 10

The gifts of prophecy

To another miraculous powers, to another prophesy, to another distinguishing between spirits, to another speaking in different kinds of tongues.

(1 Corinthians 12:10)

what is a prophecy?

Prophecy is to state what God has determined to do, immediately or in the future. It is to know the mind of God on certain issues. He may tell you why He wants to do the things He will do. Prophecies can be categorized into two parts. There are some that come directly from God, while others come indirectly. The ones that come indirectly, for example, include those that come as a sermon progresses. This is why we must always be attentive to sermons, no matter who the speaker is. Prophecy may also come through the songs during the praise and worship session.

Direct prophecy, which many of us recognize, comes when you hear, "The Lord God says…" and we know that a prophecy is coming forth.

sources of prophecy

Prophecy comes from three sources—the devil, man and God. We will examine these three sources, especially how to differentiate between them.

Demonic Prophecies

We know that Satan can prophesy through false prophets:

> And the Lord said, "Who will entice Ahab into attacking Ramoth Gilead and going to his death there?" One suggested this and another that. Finally, a spirit came forward, stood before the Lord and said "I will entice him." "By what means?" the Lord asked. "I will go out and be a lying spirit in the mouths of all his prophets," he said. "So now the Lord has put a lying spirit in the mouths of these prophets of yours. The Lord has decreed disaster for you." (1 Kings 22:20-23)

Here we meet a king whom God wanted to destroy on the battle-field, and He had to arrange this. He knew that this king would consult prophets before going to battle. God therefore sent a lying spirit into the mouth of all the prophets. It told the king to go to battle because he would win, but he went to war and was destroyed. May we never do anything that will make God decide to destroy us.

> Once when we were going to the place of prayer, we were met by a slave girl who had a spirit by which she predicted the future. She earned a great deal of money for her owners by fortune telling. This girl followed Paul and the rest of us; shouting, "These men are servants of the Most High God, who are telling you the way to be saved." (Acts 16:16-17)

This destructive spirit is called the spirit of divination; that is, it can prophesy and tell you what is likely to happen in the future. If you are not covered with the Blood of Jesus Christ, whatever this spirit says may happen to you. It may frighten you so much that the fear could kill you.

Prophets who are inspired by Satan are very wicked. Their remedies to situations do not follow the right paths but lead to destruction. They may tell you accurately what is happening or has happened in your life, but their advice will surely take you to Hell. For example, they may tell you that your wife is possessed and this could be true. However, as a solution they could recommend that you divorce your wife and marry someone else. This is against the will of God. Instead, the Holy Spirit will counsel you to cast out the demon in your wife in the name of Jesus and not to divorce her.

Satanic prophets go about their nefarious acts by delving into our "files" with Satan We all have two files—one with God and one with the devil. All the evil we ever did before we became born-again has been wiped out in our files with God, but not so with Satan. He compiled the files through his agents who followed you around when you were not a believer. When you go to psychics who seem to know everything you ever did, it's simply a ruse. They have consulted your file with Satan to see into the nook and crannies of your life, and Satan cooperates with them. So they recount your past accurately and amaze you. Obviously, in this kind of situation, if they prophesy about your future, you will believe them. But all they will prophesy will be lies and death because they cannot see into the future. Satan is a very cunning creature who drags people into his net gradually. When you go to a false prophet, like a tarot card reader or an occult meeting, whether to look into your future or for any other reason, you are gradually selling out to Satan and he will be glad to rope you in. If you want to know about your future, ask Jesus Christ instead.

Human Prophecies

Romans confirms that we have our own spirits:

> *The Spirit himself testifies with our spirit that we are God's children.* (Romans 8:16)

Our spirits can communicate with both God and Satan. The spirit in us can prophesy, especially of those things we want to hear. It normally prophesies about the good things that are pleasurable to our ears.

Jeremiah confirms that prophets who prophesy in this manner have been in existence for a long time. The text also tells us what to look out for:

> *This is what the Lord Almighty says: "Do not listen to what the prophets are prophesying to you; they fill you with false hopes. They speak visions from their own minds, not from the mouth of the Lord. They keep saying to those who despise me, 'The Lord says: You will have peace.' And to all who follow the stubbornness of their hearts they say 'No harm will come to you.'"*
>
> (Jeremiah 23:16-17)

These prophets assure liars and armed robbers that everything will be okay with them, and tell them that God said so. You cannot receive the mercy of God if you do not repent and forsake your sins. How can there be peace for a sinner? God says there is no peace for the wicked.

It is this type of prophet who tells you that someone intends to destroy you. They even go to the extent of describing the person to you and, in most cases, women are the common antagonists. But the descriptions they give of your adversaries are usually out of sync and vague, which makes you confused, suspicious of your neighbors and members of your family. These prophets foretell marriages made in Heaven after one interested party makes his or her intentions known.

Divine Prophecies

The Spirit of God also prophesies:

> *And afterward I will pour out my Spirit on all people. Your sons and daughters will prophesy, your old men*

will dream dreams, your young men will see visions.
(Joel 2:28)

God has a definitely provided for prophecy in His plans.

Three passageways for Divinely ordained prophecies

There are three channels for divinely ordained prophecies. One is through the gift of prophecy, which establishes us as God's prophets so that we can constantly hear from Him.

His word in the Bible is another surefire route through which divine prophecies come. He can illuminate a particular Bible passage in your mind. I can even tell your future from the Bible. If you are a sinner, I will tell you what Job 11:14-19 states: if you remove sin from your life, all your problems will vanish. This is prophecy because it talks about something in the future. I always rely on the fact that God talks to His people by referring them to relevant Bible passages. I know that my future will be all right because Isaiah states:

> *Tell the righteous it will be well with them, for they will enjoy the fruit of their deeds.* (Isaiah 3:10)

The future will only be well with the righteous, because you cannot be in sin and say that your future will great. If you are a sinner and you come to me and ask for a prophecy about your future, I will refer you to Isaiah, which states:

> *Woe to the wicked! Disaster is upon them! They will be paid back for what their hands have done.* (Isaiah 3:11)

You cannot remain in sin and expect that all will be well with you. It is only the grace of God that can make you prosperous and free from negative circumstances. No sinner will inherit the kingdom of God.

god, the Holy spirit

Men of God often prophesy on the basis of the word of God that is already written. We have an example in Kings:

Now Elijah the Tishbite from Tishbe in Gilead said to Ahab, "As the Lord the God of Israel lives whom I serve there will be neither dew nor rain in the next few years except at my word." (1 Kings 17:1)

This is a prophecy. Elijah must have been inspired by the Holy Spirit of God, with due reference to Deuteronomy:

Be careful or you will be enticed to turn away and worship other gods and bow down to them. Then the Lord's anger will burn against you and he will shut the heavens so that it will not rain and the ground will yield no produce and you will soon perish from the good land the Lord is giving you. (Deuteronomy 11:16-17)

At this time, Ahab and the Israelites were wantonly worshipping other gods, including Baal. Elijah relied on the word of God that never fails, to prophesy in the presence of Ahab, and it came to pass. Elijah did not call for rain again until they repented.

In 1 Kings 18:41, Elijah prophesied that rain would fall. How did he get this information? The Spirit of God must have referred him to what is written in 2 Chronicles:

When I shut up the heavens so that there is no rain or command locusts to devour the land or send a plague among my people, if my people who are called by my name will humble themselves and pray and seek my face and turn from their wicked ways, then I will hear from heaven and will forgive their sin and will heal their land. (2 Chronicles 7:13-14)

The Lord made a merciful provision for the restoration of his people. On Mount Carmel, the Israelites repented of their sins and accepted that the Lord is the Almighty when fire fell from Heaven.

Obviously, Elijah relied on this information and prophesied accordingly.

There is a particular purpose for the gift of prophecy:

> *But everyone who prophesies speaks to men for their strengthening, encouragement and comfort.*
> (1 Corinthians 14:3)

Sometimes when the people of God feel that God is far away from them, God sends a prophecy. There was a time in our congregation when God sent a word that some people wanted to commit suicide. We called them out and we prayed for them. We are sure that this brought them comfort and joy. Jeremiah tells us another purpose of prophecy:

> *If at any time I announce that a nation or kingdom is to be uprooted, torn down and destroyed and if that nation I warned repents of its evil, then I will relent and not inflict on it the disaster I had planned.*
> (Jeremiah 18:7-8)

God may warn a nation through prophecy. Any nation that forgets God will be in serious trouble, but one that turns to God will be mightily blessed. God says that if He has purposed to destroy a nation and it repents, He will forgive them.

characteristics of true prophecies

True prophecies will always come to pass, no matter how improbable they may sound. Almost all the prophecies from God have prerequisites, but when prophecies are pronounced, people do not listen to the conditions. They only want to hear the beautiful parts.

Every true prophecy must be in agreement with God's words. Any prophet who tells you to contradict the word of God to prosper is a prophet from Hell. Any prophet who says the Lord approves a second wife is a prophet from Hell.

A true prophecy must be an open matter. There is nothing secret as far as God is concerned. If a prophet tells you something and says you are not to tell anyone, you must turn away. The Bible teaches us that when people are prophesying, others must judge whether or not it is a true prophecy. God has nothing to hide.

To know whether a prophecy is true, you must find out whether or not the prophet delivering the message is pure. You can judge them by their fruits. I heard of a certain "prophet" who got six members of his congregation pregnant, and he still gets up to say, "Thus saith the Lord"! Only a fool would believe him. You must ask him which Lord he is talking about.

You must be on your guard against any prophecy that has no connection to the Gospel of Jesus Christ. The book of Revelation also helps us pinpoint true prophecies:

> At this I fell at his feet to worship him. But he said to me, "Do not do it. I am a fellow servant with you and with your brothers who hold to the testimony of Jesus. Worship God! For the testimony of Jesus is the spirit of prophecy." (Revelation 19:10)

Also note that Jesus Christ is never critical. He is always gentle, even when you have done something wrong.

> O Jerusalem, Jerusalem, you who kill the prophets and stone those sent to you, how often I have longed to gather your children together as a hen gathers her chicks under her wings, but you were not willing. Look, your house is left to you desolate. For I tell you, you will not see me again until you say, "Blessed is he who comes in the name of the Lord." (Matthew 23:37-39)

This prophecy was sent to those who had been killing prophets, yet Jesus spoke to them gently. The Bible even tells us that He was weeping while delivering this message. He said this so that they could repent, so He could accept them into the kingdom of God.

How to identify a false prophet

A false prophet always opposes the truth of God. His doctrine is never sound. He will not talk about sin because he does not live a holy life. And a false prophet is always, directly or indirectly, appealing for money.

How to recognize the gift of prophecy

When you have the gift, from time to time God will tell you certain things before they happen. After He has revealed these things to you, there will be a gentle insistence that you verbalize it, but God will not force you to talk.

When many of us began to operate with the gift of prophecy, we were always afraid to speak. I always advise that the moment God reveals certain things to you, write them down. You can put the paper into an envelope and when the prophecy comes to pass, go to another true man of God and tell him to open the envelope and check. This way you gradually build your confidence until the time when you know for sure that God has spoken. Then you will feel no hesitation or fear to speak out. However, from time to time when the Lord tells you something, you must know that there are other people who can judge better than yourself. As a beginner, you may not hear correctly what God is saying.

When do people get the gift of prophecy?

When people praise God, the Holy Spirit moves and distributes gifts that include the gift of prophecy. Do you want it? If you are not yet born again, it's not for you. Decide today to give your life to Christ and, in the not-too-distant future, God could give you this gift.

chapter 11

The Gifts of Diverse Tongues and Interpretation of Tongues

To another miraculous powers, to another prophesy, to another distinguishing between spirits, to another speaking in different kinds of tongues.

(1 Corinthians 12:10)

Tongues are Vocal Miracles

Speaking in diverse kinds of tongues has nothing to do with linguistic ability. They are supernatural utterances by the Holy Spirit in languages never learned by the speaker. Usually, the speaker and even the listeners do not understand what he or she is saying. The only one who would understand is someone with the gift of the interpretation of tongues. Therefore, the gift of speaking in diverse tongues and the gift of interpreting them complement each other, since when we speak in diverse tongues there should be someone able to interpret them.

Speaking in tongues is one of the identifying marks God gave to believers:

*And these signs will accompany those who believe: In
my name they will drive out demons; they will speak in
new tongues.* (Mark 16:17)

In the Old Testament, there was no mention of speaking in diverse
tongues except when God confused the languages of those who
were building the tower of Babel. Also, during the lifetime of Jesus
Christ, He never spoke in tongues. If He prayed in tongues, it must
have been in secret. Therefore, for His followers, these gifts fulfill
His promise that we shall do greater things than He did.

*For this reason anyone who speaks in a tongue should
pray that he may interpret what he says.*
(1 Corinthians 14:13)

It is good to be able to speak in tongues but it is better if you are
able to interpret. It is always a great pleasure when the Holy Spirit
is moving in a gathering of the children of God and somebody
stands to give the message of God in tongues. It becomes more
exciting when another person stands up to give the interpretation.

Tongues are not primarily for teaching or preaching. They are for
private devotion between human beings and God. Paul said:

*I thank God that I speak in tongues more than all of
you. But in the church I would rather speak five intel-
ligible words to instruct others than ten thousand
words in a tongue.* (1 Corinthians 14: 18-19)

Paul was saying that it is better to talk to people in a language they
understand. Paul went on to say:

*If anyone speaks in a tongue, two or at the most three
should speak, one at a time and someone must interpret. If there is no interpreter, the speaker should keep
quiet in the church and speak to himself and God.*
(1 Corinthians 14:27-28)

When there is no interpreter, do not speak in tongues. Repeat what God said to you in a language that others will understand.

The purpose of Tongues and interpretation

One of the main reasons God gives this gift is because it makes praying continually possible. Jesus said we should pray without ceasing. (1 Thessalonians 5:17) I know that it becomes difficult if you have to pray within your understanding all the time, when praying without ceasing, and there is a very little span you can cover. When we pray in tongues, the Holy Spirit will take care of the things that we cannot remember. The secret to praying for several hours at a time is to do so in tongues. Paul said:

> *For if I pray in tongues my spirit prays but my mind is unfruitful. So what shall I do? I will pray in my spirit but I will also pray with my mind; I will sing with my spirit but I will also sing with my mind.*
> (1 Corinthians 14:14-15)

Paul was saying that if he prayed in the language that he understood and became tired, he would change to speaking in tongues. When you pray in tongues, you solve the problem of your mind wandering. It does not matter where your mind is; you would have already left behind the level of the mind. Your spirit will just keep on going. It is a wonderful thing to be able to pray in the spirit.

Another major reason for this gift is to make available a special access or a secret code between you and God.

> *In the law it is written: "Through men of strange tongues and through the lips of foreigners I will speak to this people but even then they will not listen to me." says the Lord. Tongues then are a sign not for believers but for unbelievers; prophecy, however is for believers not for unbelievers. (1 Corinthians 14: 21-22)*

When I speak to God in tongues, no one else can understand what we are saying. Tongues could be given as a secret code when God wants to reveal His mind to His servant only. Of course, with His permission, the mysteries so learned could be revealed while preaching the Gospel.

> *However as it is written: "No eye has seen no ear has heard no mind has conceived what God has prepared for those who love him." But God has revealed it to us by his Spirit. The Spirit searches all things even the deep things of God.* (1 Corinthians 2:9-10)

At times, God can show you certain things and ask you to reveal them when you are preaching. Paul says:

> *Pray also for me that when I open my mouth words may be given to me so that I will fearlessly make known the mystery of the gospel.* (Ephesians 6:19)

Often you hear great things from God that are very difficult to say to others. Many times, a preacher is asked to preach an unpleasant sermon, which no one likes to do. It takes the boldness of the Holy Spirit to be able to tell people the things God wants them to hear. The moment you get the gift of tongues, you must be ready for such assignments. If you are not sure of what God has told you, seek counsel from the elders.

God wants us to grow in the spirit as we grow in age. Luke says concerning John the Baptist:

> *And he will go on before the Lord in the spirit and power of Elijah to turn the hearts of the fathers to their children and the disobedient to the wisdom of the righteous—to make ready a people prepared for the Lord.* (Luke 1:17)

In other words, even as John the Baptist was growing in the body, he was also growing in the spirit. Concerning Jesus Christ, Luke states:

And the child grew and became strong; he was filled with wisdom and the grace of God was upon him.
(Luke 2:40)

As Jesus was growing physically, He was also growing in the spirit. Anyone who is growing older without corresponding spiritual maturity is still a baby as far as God is concerned. The growth that God recognizes is growth in the spirit.

Brothers, I could not address you as spiritual but as worldly—mere infants in Christ. I gave you milk not solid food for you were not yet ready for it. Indeed you are still not ready. (1 Corinthians 3:1-2)

Paul was saying that they had been Christians for years but, because they refused to grow in spirit, they were still babies. Even today, some people are in the same spiritual position they were when they became born-again years earlier. Some are not yet baptized in the Holy Spirit. Some have been baptized in the Holy Spirit but they have never spoken in tongues. They remain babies. When they fall ill, they run to the pastor. When they should be praying for others, they are being prayed for because they are spiritually stagnant. Only when you grow in the spirit can you experience the power of the Almighty God.

How can we grow in the spirit?

But dear friends, remember what the apostles of our Lord Jesus Christ foretold. They said to you, "In the last times there will be scoffers who will follow their own ungodly desires." These are the men who divide you who follow mere natural instincts and do not have the Spirit. But you dear friends build yourselves up in your most holy faith and pray in the Holy Spirit.
(Jude 17-20)

Paul is saying that some people want to keep on growing. We can grow by praying in tongues.

Another reason God gives the gift of tongues is to get us out of difficult situations. God can supernaturally help you understand the language of others. There's the story of an American preacher who went to Spain to preach. On the day he was to speak, his interpreter was nowhere to be found. He was in a tight spot, so he called on God for help. God responded by giving him the power to speak in the Spanish language, which he never understood before then.

There's another true story of a midwife in the Church Maternity Center who had to attend to a woman whose language she did not understand. The patient also did not understand her language. The midwife called on God, who responded by giving her utterance in the language of the patient for as long as the patient stayed at the center. Our God works in mysterious ways.

The gift of the interpretation of tongues could be given to bring glory to God among the heathen, as in Daniel 5 when only Daniel could interpret the writing on the wall. God was showing the people present that He alone knew the meaning of all things.

> *This man Daniel whom the king called Belteshazzar was found to have a keen mind and knowledge and understanding and also the ability to interpret dreams explain riddles and solve difficult problems. Call for Daniel and he will tell you what the writing means.*
>
> (Daniel 5:12)

At the end of that episode, God was glorified. But the greatest reason why God gives this gift is to prepare us for Heaven.

> *All of them were filled with the Holy Spirit and began to speak in other tongues as the Spirit enabled them. Now there were staying in Jerusalem, god-fearing Jews from every nation under Heaven. When they heard this sound a crowd came together in bewilderment because each one heard them speaking in his own language. Utterly amazed they asked, "Are not all these men who*

are speaking Galileans? Then how is it that each of us hears them in his own native language?" (Acts 2:4-8)

In this instance, people from different nations were able to understand each other. When we get to Heaven, we will be speaking in different languages but we will be understood. What else can be as beautiful as that? How lovely Heaven will be! To know this, you have to get there. To get there, you have to be born-again. The choice is yours.

chapter 12

The gift of faith

To another faith by the same Spirit, to another gifts of healing by that one Spirit. (1 Corinthians 12:9)

Faith is an acknowledgment that God exists and that He is holy and supreme. In fact, faith is the engine that drives the other gifts of the Holy Spirit. Hebrews gives us the definition of faith:

And without faith it is impossible to please him; because anyone who comes to him must believe that he exists and that he rewards those who earnestly seek him. (Hebrews 11:6)

We must do everything based on faith. We pray because we believe that there is a God that answers prayers. We want to be saved because we believe that there is a God that saves souls. We want to go to Heaven because we believe that Heaven is God's home. We say we do not want to go to Hell because we believe that Hell is the place for the enemies of God. We want to live holy because we know that this is what God wants. Everything comes back to God. A person who does not have faith in God does not have faith in anything else. And anyone who believes there is a God already has faith.

god, the Holy spirit

Now faith is being sure of what we hope for and certain of what we do not see. (Hebrews 11:1)

I know that there is a God who has all powers, who remains the same. I know that I will get well if I pray to God when I am sick because I know that there is a God. I know that my future is secure in Jesus Christ. The ultimate confidence of the Christian faith is simply that God exists.

what is the foundation of faith?

The foundation of our faith is that God is holy. A Holy God cannot lie. If He lies then He is no longer God. If He is no longer God, then everything in this Universe will collapse. If God tells a lie just once, the sun and the moon will shift positions and all the stars will scatter. The world will cease to be. If God changes for a moment, everything will collapse. Without a doubt, God is holy.

When it seems that things are not going as we expect and confusion sets in, what gives us peace is that God is holy and He is forever on His throne. He cannot be overthrown and is never confused. Before you get to Heaven, you will undergo some obstacles and discomforts, but God is only interested in finished products. The piece of wood that will become fine furniture must be ready for some rough sandpaper sessions. When things get tough, do not let your faith fluctuate.

Common or Natural Faith

This is common to believers and non-believers alike. It is the inborn faith that is demonstrated in everyday living. For example, in an auditorium full of chairs, you would sit without checking to see if the seat was there, simply believing that you would not fall. This is an act of faith that we all take for granted It is this type of faith that sees you through your travel by air because you believe the plane will not crash, even though you do not have the faintest idea how an airplane flies. Some people even trust the pilot more than they trust God. They believe the pilot will take them to their destination but they are not sure whether Jesus Christ will take them to Heaven.

Faith in God

This is the faith that allows you to believe what is yet to happen as if it has already happened. We will discuss this in greater details as we go on.

Little Faith

Jesus Christ talks about little faith:

> *If that is how God clothes the grass of the field which is here today and tomorrow is thrown into the fire will he not much clothe you. O you of little faith?*
>
> (Matthew 6:30)

Growing Faith

No matter how little faith you have, it can grow. The more you hear the message of God, the more your faith grows. The Apostles asked Jesus to increase their faith:

> *The apostles said to the Lord, "Increase our faith!"*
>
> (Luke 17:5)

Great Faith

This is the type of faith that the Centurion demonstrated in Matthew:

> *When Jesus heard this, he was astonished and said to those following him, "I tell you the truth, I have not found anyone in Israel with such great faith."*
>
> (Matthew 8:10)

Mustard Seed Faith

Jesus Christ said that faith as small as a mustard seed can move mountains:

> *Then the disciples came to Jesus in private and asked, "Why couldn't we drive it out?" He replied, "Because you have so little faith. I tell you the truth, if you have faith as small as a mustard seed, you can say to this mountain, 'Move from here to there' and it will move. Nothing will be impossible for you."*
>
> (Matthew 17:19- 20)

Faith as a Fruit of the Holy Spirit

Galatians showcases this type of faith:

> *But the fruit of the Spirit is love, joy peace, patience, kindness, goodness, faithfulness.* (Galatians 5:22)

This is the faith that gives us peace and makes us believe in the promises of God. It assures us that we are healed because the Bible tells us that by His stripes we are healed. Those who have this kind of faith do not question the actions of God. They believe that everything works out for the best so they are at peace. It was this type of faith that Peter had when he was in Herod's prison. He was at peace. The angel that came to deliver him found him fast asleep. It was this type of faith that made Jesus Christ sleep in the face of the storm, (Luke 8) God has given to everyone a measure of faith:

> *For by the grace given me I say to every one of you: Do not think of yourself more highly than you ought but rather think of yourself with sober judgment in accordance with the measure of faith God has given you.*
>
> (Romans 12:3)

Some of us have allowed our faith to grow while others have doused the fire of their faith for one reason or another. For example, wrong doctrines and false teachings can kill your faith.

> *Avoid godless chatter because those who indulge in it will become more and more ungodly. Their teaching will spread like gangrene. Among them are Hymenaeus and Philetus, who have wandered away from the truth. They say that the resurrection has already taken place and they destroy the faith of some.*
> (2 Timothy 2:16-18)

Many Christians have remained poor because they have been taught that a Christian must not be rich. They claim Jesus Christ said it was difficult for a rich person to get into Heaven, therefore they believe they must be poor. The Bible clearly states that Jesus said those who adore riches would always find it difficult to become saved. The believer's wealth is meant for God's purposes.

Some preachers say healing is against God's will because he wants you to carry your cross if you are ill. They preach that sickness is a cross. I do not know where this is in the Bible. The devil is the author of sickness, not God. We have been healed by the stripes of Jesus Christ.

False teachings can kill your faith while the truth can increase your faith. Faith comes by hearing the word of God, but it can falter under great stress. Adversity makes faith fade at times, when things look confused and it seems there is no way out. This in fact happened to John the Baptist:

> *When John heard in prison what Christ was doing he sent his disciples to ask him, "Are you the one who was to come or should we expect someone else?"*
> (Matthew 11:2-3)

John wondered whether Jesus Christ knew that he was in prison. He became downcast and his faith wavered, even though he had shouted at the River Jordan that Jesus Christ was the Messiah. I pray that your faith will never dwindle. Always remember that God is holy and He reigns forever.

There may be occasions in your life when the storms are very great and it will seem as if God is nowhere to be found. You will be tempted to doubt whether God exists. I want you to know that God is not only alive but he is always in control. It does not matter what happens, He is on His throne ruling His entire creation. He answers our prayers.

faith, the fruit is different from faith, the gift

The type of faith that is the fruit of the Holy Spirit is quiet and restful. It produces a peaceful confidence within the believer that all will be well, and he will never question God. Romans gives a classic description of this type of faith:

> Oh the depth of the riches of the wisdom and knowledge of God! How unsearchable his judgments and his paths beyond tracing out! Who has known the mind of the Lord? Or who has been his counselor? Who has ever given to God that God should repay him? For from him and through him and to him are all things. To him be glory forever! Amen. (Romans 11:33-36)

It is this type of faith that kept Elijah for one year by Brook Cherith. It rescued the widow of Zarephath and her son from famine. (1 Kings 17:8-16)

> Though he slay me yet will I hope in him I will surely defend my ways to his face. (Job 13:15)

Job said he would trust God even if it cost him his life. He said he would not do anything that would make God angry and that he would never deny God. Job was better at the end than at the beginning. If only we can trust God, He will take care of us.

On the other hand, faith as the gift of the Holy Spirit is active and dynamic. It is like a bulldozer in nature, and it works like lightning. It shuts the mouths of lions and turns a fiery furnace into an air-conditioned room. It is the faith that makes angels run helter-skelter to see that the demand and petition of the believer are met. It subdues kingdoms, and is the type of faith you need to fight the devil and his demons. It is an aggressive type of faith.

> *And what more shall I say? I do not have time to tell about Gideon, Barak, Samson, Jephtath, David, Samuel and the prophets; who through faith conquered kingdoms, administered justice and gained what was promised; who shut the mouths of lions, quenched the fury of the flames and escaped the edge of the sword; whose weakness was turned to strength and who became powerful in battle and routed foreign armies. Women received back their dead raised to life again. Others were tortured and refused to be released so that they might gain a better resurrection.*
>
> (Hebrews 11:32-35)

This faith is not the type that sits down and allows things to happen any way they will. It does not take "no" for an answer, and it fights sicknesses. It is the type of faith the devil does not mess with.

The cornerstone of faith is the holiness of god

The foundation of this type of faith is the belief that God is holy.

> *The grass withers and the flowers fall, but the word of our God stands forever.* (Isaiah 40:8)

It is true that the word of God and His promises stand forever. The foundation of faith is the unchangeable Word of God.

What gives us the assurance of healing when we pray for the sick? The word of God. It says by Jesus' stripes we have been healed. (Isaiah 53:5; 1 Peter 2:24) Some people wonder how His stripes can heal, but if they do not, then God is no longer true. For more than twenty-three years now I have relied on Jesus Christ for my healing and I enjoy divine health.

What gives us confidence and peace of mind in the face of famine and economic doom? The word of God states that He will supply in full all our needs. (Philippians 4:19) His word promises that He will provide for all my needs: physical, material, financial, academic and spiritual.

> *The lions may grow weak and hungry but those who seek the Lord lack no good thing.* (Psalm 34:10)

Are you seeking God? If so, then you will never lack any good thing.

> *For the Lord God is a sun and shield, the Lord bestows favor and honor; no good thing does he withhold from those whose walk is blameless.* (Psalm 84:11)

Are you anxious about tomorrow? Your future will surely be all right as long as you are with Jesus Christ and live a holy life.

> *Blessed is the man who does not walk in the counsel of the wicked or stand in the way of sinners or seat in the seat of mockers. But his delight is in the law of the Lord and on his law he meditates day and night. He is like a tree planted by streams of water, which yields its fruit in season and whose leaf does not wither. Whatever he does prospers.* (Psalm 1:1-3)

How can the tree by the riverside be worried about remaining green? Whether it rains or not, the tree will be nourished. If you are on the side of Jesus Christ, wherever you go and whatever you do, He will take care of you. All the great men of faith such as Daniel, Elijah, Shadrach, Meshach and Abednego based their faith on the word of God. Let us take a closer look at the travails of Shadrach, Meshach and Abednego. These three made a bold statement with bold faith:

> If we are thrown into the blazing furnace, the God we serve is able to save us from it and he will rescue us from your hand, O King. (Daniel 3:17)

How did they know that God would deliver them from the fiery furnace? Not because He had delivered someone from a fiery furnace before. But they remembered the word of God:

> When you pass through the waters I will be with you and when you pass through the rivers they will not sweep over you. When you walk through the fire you will not be burned; the flames will not set you ablaze.
> (Isaiah 43:2)

This promise from God gave them the assurance that He would deliver them. It assures us that if we walk through rivers, we will not get drowned. If we walk through fire, we will not be scorched. Shadrach, Meshach and Abednego knew that God always fulfills His promises. When God made this promise, He was well aware that we cannot walk through fire by ourselves, but if an enemy puts us through fire, the God we serve will surely deliver us. Isaiah gives us another promise of God:

> You will keep in perfect peace him whose mind is steadfast because he trusts in you. (Isaiah 26:3)

God says He will keep us in perfect peace if we can trust Him completely. A lot of people suffer from all sorts of diseases because they are always worried, but if God is on your side you will have no problems. He will take care of all challenges to your joy.

No harm befalls the righteous but the wicked have their fill of trouble. (Proverbs 12:21)

The moment you stop living holy, trouble begins.

why Does god give us the gift of faith?

God gives us the gift of faith for protection from evil and danger. There are two different types of danger: natural dangers such as storms and earthquakes, and danger from the forces of darkness. God protects His children from all these by giving them the gift of faith.

Dangers from the forces of darkness include evil spirits, witches and wizards. These forces watch us everyday, seeking to harm us. They are always looking for ways to overcome us.

We can also include here the hazards presented by those who do not know God, such as drunken drivers on the roads, armed robbers who insist on killing their victims, assassins and street fighters. Once you are sure that God will protect you and you believe it, He will do so. He will make sure that you are not around dangerous situations.

Surely he will save you from the fowler's snare and from the deadly pestilence. (Psalm 91:3)

God will deliver us from all sorts of sicknesses and dangers. When others are panic-stricken or afraid, the Holy Spirit will remind you:

You will not fear the terror of night nor the arrow that flies by day. (Psalm 91:5)

As a child of God, you are to sleep in peace. No evil will happen to you. Many children of God are afraid of sudden death, but this verse should minister to them:

Nor the pestilence that stalks in the darkness, nor the plague that destroys at midday. A thousand may fall at your side, ten thousand at your right hand but it will not come near you. (Psalm 91:6-7)

No sudden death shall befall me. This Psalm goes further to say that we should no longer fear Satan and his cohorts:

You will tread upon the lion and the cobra; you will trample the great lion and the serpent. (Psalm 91:13)

Snakes symbolize Satan and his agents. I will continue to trample on them and they will never overcome me. Job said:

I know that my Redeemer lives and that in the end he will stand upon the earth. And after my skin has been destroyed yet in my flesh I will see God; I myself will see him with my own eyes—I and not another, How my heart yearns within me! (Job 19:25-27)

Even in the face of his problems and tribulations, Job was sure that his Redeemer lived. As long as I know that God lives forever, I have the assurance that He knows about everything that happens to me. If He knows, then I am convinced that all things work for the good for those who love God. There is no doubt that my Redeemer lives.

God said to Moses, "I AM WHO I AM. This is what you are to say to the Israelites: I AM has sent me to you." God also said to Moses, "Say to the Israelites, The Lord, the God of your fathers—the God of Abraham, the God of Isaac and the God of Jacob—has sent me to you." This is my name forever, the name by which I am to be remembered from generation to generation."

(Exodus 3:14-15)

God is saying that He is alive forever. Job remembered that he served the I AM THAT I AM, the God whose Name will last forever.

Faith is given to people who are versed in the word of God because when trouble comes, it is the word of God that will be their foundation. You will use it as a weapon against Satan.

Furthermore, if you want the gift of faith, you must be ready to surrender everything to Jesus Christ. You must be ready to die for Him and be totally submissive to Him. The moment you receive the gift of faith, you can no longer be an ordinary Christian. You will want to fight the devil, always. Anyone who is not ready to die cannot go into battle.

chapter 13

The Gifts of Healing

To another faith by the same Spirit, to another gifts of healing by that one Spirit. (1 Corinthians 12:9)

The gift of healing has nothing to do with modern medicine. That is, we are not talking about a doctor who knows his job well. This gift is given to special people (1Cor. 12:30), although every child of God can pray for the sick without necessarily having it. Furthermore, there are gifts of healing because there are sicknesses and diseases. God has arranged different gifts to handle different illnesses.

Why God Gives us the Gifts of Healing

God gives us the gifts of healing so that the Body of Christ will be strong physically. We believers are members of the body of Christ and His bride. If any part of the body is diseased, the head will not be at peace. Jesus is our head. As long as we are suffering, Jesus Christ is suffering with us. He has released the gifts of healing so that, together with Him, we can all be well.

Secondly, Jesus wants us to be happy all the time.

Philip went down to a city in Samaria and proclaimed the Christ there. When the crowds heard Philip and saw the miraculous signs he did, they all paid close attention to what he said. With shrieks, evil spirits came out of many and many paralytics and cripples were healed. So there was great joy in that city.

(Acts 8:5-8)

Joy comes with healing. Happiness is infectious spreads when healing is received.

The third reason why God gives the gifts of healing is so that we can give Him all glory. Isaiah records someone's testimony:

For the grave cannot praise you, death cannot sing your praise; those who go down to the pit cannot hope for your faithfulness. The living, the living they praise you, as I am doing today; fathers tell their children about your faithfulness. The Lord will save me and we will sing with stringed instruments all the days of our lives in the temple of the Lord. (Isaiah 38:18-20)

It is only those who are alive and well that can praise the Lord the way He ought to be praised.

Types of Gifts of Healing

The general gift of healing deals with sicknesses caused by bacteria, germs and viruses, and can be used to cure minor illnesses. None of these can withstand the Blood of Jesus. Sickness and I cannot coexist in my body, the temple of the Almighty God. Peter, like all the other Apostles, had this gift:

As a result people brought the sick into the streets and laid them on beds and mats so that at least Peter's shadow might fall on some of them as he passed by. Crowds gathered also from the towns around

Jerusalem, bringing their sick and those tormented by
evil spirits and all of them were healed. (Acts 5:15-16)

A higher gift of healing is used to cast out the demons that cause
blindness, deafness and dumbness. Some people are deaf or blind
for physical reasons, others for spiritual ones.

When someone is blind and his eyes are still open, the problem is
not because of physical damage done to the eyes but a demon that
has stolen the sight. If you cast out the demon, the fellow will
begin to see immediately. There are those who are deaf because
there are demons blocking their ear drums, while others are mute
because demons are holding on to their vocal cords. We have an
example of this in Matthew:

When evening came many who were demon possessed
were brought to him and he drove out the spirits with
a word and healed all the sick. (Matthew 8:16)

There is another category of sickness that is even more difficult,
but also connected to demon activity. Some demons are easier to
handle than others. Ephesians confirms this:

For our struggle is not against flesh and blood, but
against the rulers, against the authorities, against the
powers of this dark world and against the spiritual
forces of evil in the heavenly realms. (Ephesians 6:12)

The epileptic demon is one of the worst, as we see in Matthew:

Then the disciples came to Jesus in private and asked,
"Why couldn't we drive it out?" He replied, "Because
you have so little faith. I tell you the truth, if you have
faith as small as a mustard seed, you can say to this
mountain 'Move from here to there' and it will move.
Nothing will be impossible for you."

(Matthew 17:19-21)

The disciples could not handle this epileptic case. Jesus explained why they couldn't cure it even though they had been casting out demons before. (Luke 10:17) Jesus told them the key was fasting and prayers. That's the way to deal with evil powers. No matter how great your gift might be, if you do not fast and pray, there are some demons that you will never be able to defeat. Although the Holy Spirit does the work, it is essential that the vessel to be used by the Holy Spirit be primed for maximum effectiveness.

There is yet a higher gift of healing that returns health to dead parts of the bodies; for example, blindness not caused by demons. In such cases, God must create new parts. John 9 provides an example of this when we meet a man who was born blind. Jesus spit on the ground, made some mud and remolded the eye again. This case was also used as an example to glorify God.

The gift that I consider the very highest is the one that raises the dead. This is, without doubt, a miracle. In raising the dead, as we have in the case of Lazarus, three things need to happen. First, the dead body and blood must be revived. Second, the spirit must return into the body. And third, the cause of death must be eliminated. What gladdens my heart is that it is not only Jesus who has this gift; Peter had it and he raised Dorcas from the dead. (Acts 9:40) You too can have it.

conditions for receiving the gifts of Healing

First and foremost, to receive the gifts of healing you must be born-again. If you are not born-again, how can God use you? To attempt healing without being born again is to attack your master, since anyone who is not a believer belongs to the devil and the devil is responsible for all sicknesses. He can never tolerate one of his own casting out demons. This is why witch doctors and those who practice occult healing procedures are all tricksters. When you consult them to get a cure for headache, you may seem to be cured but you get a stomachache in return. This way they save face with Satan by still keeping you in bondage.

Sanctification is a must for a believer, and it is compulsory to be baptized in the power of the Holy Spirit to receive the gift. If you lack any of these three prerequisites, ask God for them *before* you launch your quest for the gifts of healing.

Another necessary qualifier for the gift of healing is mercy. Unkind people cannot receive this gift, no matter how much they fast or pray. We must not forget that these gifts are the sole preserve of the Holy Spirit and he gives them out as he pleases. The Bible tells us that those who have received mercy from the Lord are candidates for other good gifts, and in Matthew 5:7 we are told that the merciful will receive mercy. Mercy and compassion brought out the healing gift in Jesus Christ when He was on earth. Many women have been used mightily in the healing ministry, because they are tender people. I have decided to cultivate this attitude of mercy. God is ready to use anyone of us if mercy is flowing in us.

Any one who wants the gift of healing must be resolute in his or her goals. Apostle Peter is a good example. When Jesus Christ was arrested in the garden of Gethsemane, Peter took his sword and cut off the ear of the high priest's servant in defense of the man he believed in. Jesus restored the man's ear and commanded Peter to put away the sword. Then our Lord Jesus conceded to his detractors, who took him to Pontius Pilate's court. Peter doggedly followed at a distance.

Saul of Tarsus was also a stubborn person, passionate whether he was right or wrong. After the assassination plot against Stephen was sealed, he was determined to see that the stoning was carried out. Later he became Paul the Apostle, who faced many assassination attempts on his life including a stoning siege. Once he was stoned, he fainted yet he went on preaching the gospel of Christ.

People with this type of determination receive the gifts of healing for two reasons. First, those who waiver cannot be trusted. So, God will not bestow the gifts of healing on them. If you are not determined to follow God forever, you will not receive anything from Him. The second is that anyone who has the gifts of healing is Satan's number one enemy. This gift arouses satanic opposition. You put Satan to shame and threaten his existence anytime you use the gifts of healing.

To receive this gift, you must be a very zealous person. We have the example of Peter:

> Simon answered, "Master we've worked hard all night and haven't caught anything, but because you say so, I will let down the nets." (Luke 5:5)

Peter was a fisherman. He labored and toiled all the night and very early in the morning when Jesus told him to cast out his net, he did so simply because he was eager to obey Jesus. God does not use lazy people. You cannot have the gift of healing without people seeking you out, which keeps you alert and busy all the time. If you are not devoted, do not ask for the gifts of healing.

нow to use the gift

If you have the gifts of healing, you must remember that healing is food for the children and not for dogs. (Matthew 15:25-27) So it is essential that you tell anyone who comes to you for healing about salvation, to convert the person from the position of a dog to that of a child. When this is taken care of, healing and victory will come. This is why we have a lot of healing during crusades— once people give their lives to Jesus Christ, it becomes easier for them to be healed.

You must boost the faith of the sick since healing comes by faith. Unless the sick have the assurance that Jesus will heal them, they will not be healed. You must make it known to the sick person that you are not their healer; the Lord Jesus Christ is.

As the power of healing is coming from the person praying, the person who wants healing must be ready to receive it. They must take a step of faith. Jesus healed a bed-ridden paralytic as He said:

> *"But so that you may know that the son of man has power on earth to forgive sins..." Then he said to the paralytic, "Get up, take your mat and go home."*
>
> (Matthew 9:6)

Jesus merely wanted him to exercise his faith. Matthew recounts the story of the man with a shriveled hand that could not be moved. Yet Jesus said he should stretch his hands out and the man did so, completely healed in the process.

> *Then he said to the man, "Stretch out your hand." So he stretched it out and it was completely restored, just as sound as the other.* (Matthew 12:13)

The man took a step of faith and his hand was healed. You must tell the sick that God wants to heal them and they should be ready to receive. Encourage them to try to do what they couldn't do before. God will heal them because God is faithful.

The gift of healing is not magic or show business. Any time you lay hands on the sick and they recover, a great fight is going on between God and Satan. As you minister to the sick the devil tries to draw the person you are praying for away from God. When people challenge you to use your gift of healing, tell them that you and the gift are not for display at their beck and call. Here's how Jesus reacted to that situation:

> *Then some of the Pharisees and teachers of the law said to him, "Teacher, we want to see a miraculous sign from you." He answered, "A wicked and adulterous generation asks for a miraculous sign! But none will be given it except the sign of the prophet Jonah."*
>
> (Matthew 12:38-39)

If you are given the gift of healing and you become proud, God will withdraw it.

You must tell the sick that healing can come gradually but it will surely come. Not all healings are instant, although many people want it to be. Once you have prayed and said "Amen" the power is instant, but the manifestation of the healing may not come immediately. Once the sick person agrees with you that the healing has taken place, though, nothing can stop it, no matter how much Satan threatens. However, the working of miracles does happen without delay. This is why it is different from the gifts of healing.

> *As he was going into a village, ten men who had leprosy met him. They stood at a distance and called out in a loud voice, "Jesus, Master have pity on us!" When he saw them, he said, "Go, show yourselves to the priests." And as they went they were cleansed.*
>
> (Luke 17:12-14)

They were not cleansed the instant Jesus spoke to them. Jesus can heal instantly if He wants to, but He can also heal gradually. You must explain this to those who need healing so they understand that if healing does not happen immediately, they are not to lose hope.

The gift of healing should not be used indiscriminately. You must allow the spirit of God to guide you in how to use it. Do not be in a hurry to lay hands on any sick person without the Holy Spirit leading you. Some people come to Jesus just to take advantage of His healing power. Once they are healed, they go back into the world to do their own thing. If you pray for this kind of person, God, who knows the end from the beginning, may not answer your prayers and you may be discouraged.

Jesus did not heal all whom he came across:

> *Now there is in Jerusalem near the Sheep gate, a pool; which in Aramaic is called Bethesda and which is surrounded by five covered colonnades. Here a great num-*

ber of disabled people used to lie, the blind, the lame,
the paralyzed. One who was there had been an invalid
for thirty-eight years. (John 5:2,3,5)

There were many people beside the pool, but Jesus went to only
one of them. Immediately He healed him, then He left the place.
Why did He not heal the others? Let us look at Luke:

And there were many in Israel with leprosy in the time
of Elisha the prophet, yet only one of them was
cleansed, only Naaman the Syrian. (Luke 4:27)

Only God knows why this is so. The important thing is for God to
delight Himself in our lives so that He heals those He wants to
heal through us.

If you have the gifts of healing, you must continue to be fervent in
prayer and fasting. There are three major reasons for this. First,
we are all trying to follow the example of Jesus Christ. Almost anytime He healed a lot of people, He would spend the following night
praying. Secondly, fasting will bring your body under submission
so that you will not become a cast away in the future. Fasting subdues your body and keeps you from becoming proud. And finally,
Heaven is our goal. You may perform miracles, signs and wonders
in this world and still fail to make it to Heaven. Even if you have
no gifts at all, your priority should always be to go to Heaven.

If you are not born-again, God will not give you the gifts of healing. If you are already born- again, before you ask for the gifts, ask
God to heal you of every sickness in your body. Then you can ask
for the gift of healing others.

chapter 14

The gift of
working of miracles

To another miraculous powers, to another prophesy, to another distinguishing between spirits, to another speaking in different kinds of tongues.

(1 Corinthians 12:10)

what is a miracle?

In this world, there are certain physical laws that direct our lives. For example, there is a law against stealing and a law against murder. There are other types of laws like the law of gravity, which states that whatever goes up must surely come down. Just as we have laws in the physical world, we have laws in the spiritual world that regulate things in that realm.

Some of the laws in the spiritual world have equivalents in the physical world, such as the law of harvest. In the physical world, you will reap whatever you sow. If you plant maize, there is no amount of fertilizer that can convert your yield to yams. In spiritual law as well, you will reap whatever you sow.

Do not be deceived, God is not mocked. A man sows what he reaps. The one who sows to please his nature, from that nature will reap destruction; the one who sows to please the Spirit, from the Spirit will reap eternal life. Let us not become weary in doing good, for at the proper time we will reap a harvest if we do not give up. (Galatians 6:7-9)

The law of harvest also states that you will reap more than you have sown. If you plant a corn seed during the planting season, by harvest time you will definitely reap more than the seed planted. The same happens in the spiritual realm, but spiritual laws are more powerful than physical laws and can control them. You may see someone become ill quickly without any apparent physical cause, when in truth something is happening to that person in the spiritual realm.

Just as the judgment passed by the court can be set aside by the Supreme Court, so can spiritual laws overrule all physical laws. For example, in the physical realm there is the law of death that says anyone who dies will remain dead. However, in the spiritual realm there is the law of resurrection that dictates that the dead shall rise again. The law of resurrection is superior to the law of death.

Jesus said to her, "Your brother will rise again." Martha answered, "I know he will rise again in the resurrection at the last day." Jesus said to her, "I am the resurrection and the life. He who believes in me will live, even though he dies and whoever lives and believes in me will never die. Do you believe this?" (John 11:23-26)

Jesus acknowledged that there was a law of death, but told Martha that He had come to put aside that law. He applied the law of resurrection when He raised Lazarus from the dead.

The law of resurrection is also stronger than the law of gravity, as we see after Jesus rose from the dead:

After this he was taken up before their very eyes and a cloud hid him from their sight. (Acts 1:9)

Normally, no one can go up without falling down. When the law of resurrection begins to work in your life, you will keep on rising. It is the law of resurrection that will lift us up to join Jesus Christ in the clouds when He comes back, and it enabled Jesus walk on water. The law of gravity is actually stopped because Jesus is the Resurrection and the Life. On the day Jesus ascended into Heaven, the law of resurrection was in full display.

I have gone into details on these laws so you can understand the meaning of miracles. Miracles occur when a spiritual law over-rules a physical law to make something unusual happen. Jesus Christ is the superintendent of spiritual laws and God is the One behind every miracle. It is wrong to say that the days of miracles are long gone, because it is not history that performs miracles. God has always been in the miracle business because He is still alive and never ceases to be Himself. And certainly Jesus is the same as the Father.

Jesus Christ is the same yesterday and today and for-ever. (Hebrews 13:8)

As long as Jesus Christ remains on His throne, miracles will continue to happen. They do so all the time.

How does God work miracles? He can use natural means, as when Jesus wanted to feed some people in John 6:5-6. He used the things the world was familiar with—five loaves of bread and two fishes. In the physical law of hunger, this food is enough for just one boy. Jesus Christ applied the spiritual law of provision and it became more than enough for many thousands.

Another example is the widow in 2 Kings 4:1-7. God could have provided money in a spectacular way. He could have turned stones into money. Rather, as the sovereign Lord of the entire universe, He decided to use what the woman had to make her rich. God used the little oil that she had to provide for her needs and that of her children. God used the spiritual law of multiplication, which makes a mighty ocean out of a little drop of water.

Miracles happen every day. The problem is that we are so materially minded that we usually cannot see spiritual things. For example, the water that oranges and grapes take in from the soil is being changed into "wine," as it were, every day. It is the water that the plants take from the ground that is changed into juice, which makes these fruits so succulent and enjoyable. When Jesus changed water into wine, people were amazed, but He is still doing it today, all over the world. I believe that if you hand over whatever you have to Jesus Christ, He will perform a miracle with it and through it. Those who know God in this way know how to give to Him. You are merely handing what is physical to Him so He can apply His own spiritual laws. The result will be a miracle.

Occasionally, however, God may not use a natural method to perform a miracle. Because He is the controller of the heavens, He can use heavenly things. When God destroyed Sodom and Gomorra, He used a supernatural method: fire fell from heaven. And when He answered the prayer of Elijah on Mount Carmel, fire fell from Heaven.

Sometimes when we are expecting a miracle from God, we look at our pockets and think of our personal possessions. God doesn't need them. If He does not use physical methods, He will use supernatural methods. He does what He likes.

Types of Miracles

There are seven different types of miracles.

There are miracle supplies, as in the case of Elijah and the widow of Zarephath in 1 Kings 17. God provided for them for more than two years from just a flask of oil. A miracle resurrection was demonstrated in the life of Lazarus. God also passes miracle judgment on sinners. In Acts 5:1-5, we see the judgment on Ananias and Sapphira. If you do not want this type of miracle, you had better sever every link with sin.

There is the miracle of deliverance that cures the mentally deranged and sets people free from demons. When the law of the world has condemned you to death, only God can deliver you. Once God sets you free, no one can bind you again—as long as you do not sell yourself out.

We have miracles that overrule nature. For example, rivers naturally flow downstream. If it pleases God, He can cause the river to flow uphill or upstream. Another example was when Joshua commanded the sun to stand still in Joshua 10:11-14. There was a time when Jesus Christ went into the house where his disciples had been hiding since His death without opening the door. He visited "doubting Thomas" so he could see His pierced side and hands.

We have some miracles that are unusual, the type that happens once in a lifetime. We have many examples of this in the Bible. The Immaculate Conception of Jesus is a great miracle and it happened only once. There is also the story of Gideon who asked God for a sign of his ordination as a deliverer, as recorded in Judges 6:36-40. The signs that God gave him were never repeated after that time. Yet another example is Balaam and the talking ass. God can perform a miracle exclusively for you; He knows your problems better than anyone.

There is a peculiar type of miracle described in Deuteronomy:

> *During the forty years that I led you through the desert, your clothes did not wear out nor did the scandals on your feet.* (Deuteronomy 29:5)

The children of Israel enjoyed a forty-year preservation of their personal wardrobe through many savage seasons in the wilderness. This happened because the God of miracles walked with them. If you really love God, you can remain young forever. If He has the power to make sure that clothes continue to look new, then He must have the power to make human beings look young forever. After all, the Bible says those who wait on the Lord will renew their strength. This is an incontestable miracle.

Receiving a miracle differs from the working of miracles

There is a difference between receiving a miracle and having the gift of the working of miracles. Let's make that clear through the illustration of the baker and the bread. Simply put, receiving a loaf of bread is different from baking the bread. The one who receives a miracle can be likened to the person who receives a gift of a loaf of bread while the one who has the gift of working of miracles can be likened to one who makes the bread.

Anyone can receive a miracle from God if they have enough faith. Miracles don't just happen. "Cliff-edge" experiences, which drive people to the wall, make perfect situations for miracles to occur. When you can still provide for your own needs, you don't have to depend on God's provisions. But during a personal or national crisis, you will know how to call on the "hope of the hopeless." On the other hand, you will die of hunger when you have all the ingredients to prepare food in your kitchen and you still ask God to provide food instead.

The purpose of the gift of the working of miracles

The working of miracles is one of God's most precious gifts. When you have it, you are doing what only God can do. Of all the nine gifts it is the most sought after. God gives these gifts to solve a lot of problems. We will discuss seven of them.

God uses this gift to get his children out of sticky situations. That was the case when death stalked Elijah to the widow's house in Zarephath.

Some time later the son of the woman who owned the house became ill. He grew worse and worse and finally stopped breathing. She said to Elijah, "What do you have against me, man of God? Did you come to remind me of my sin and kill my son? "Give me your son," Elijah replied. He took him from her arms, carried him to the upper room where he was staying and laid him on his bed. Then he cried out to the Lord, "O Lord my God have you brought tragedy also upon this widow I am staying with by causing her son to die?"

(1 Kings 17:17-20)

Life-threatening circumstances led Elijah to the house of the widow of Zarephath where he became a guest. When the widow's son died, Elijah's spiritual mandate was put to the test. God allowed a miracle healing to take place. God canceled the death sentence and averted Elijah's spiritual disgrace.

God also uses this gift to decimate demonic obstructions. Any time Satan tries to hinder you, God puts the gift of the working of miracles to work. An example is found in Acts 13:6-12. While Paul was preaching to a governor, there was a representative of Satan there called Elymas, who tried to oppose the preaching of the Gospel and prevent Governor Sergius Paulus from believing. Paul used the gift of the working of miracles to strike him blind and the governor's soul was saved. Remember that Satan can use human beings to impede your progress.

The gift of the working of miracles is one of the weapons God has given men of God for the enforcement of discipline in the body of Christ. A pastor is powerless in the face of flagrant disobedience by his congregation. But those who understand divine authority will listen, particularly to true men of God. A biblical case in point is the disciplinary measures meted out to Gehazi by Elisha. (2 Kings 5:26-27) He simply spoke and Gehazi became a leper instantly. The gift of the working of miracles almost invariably works through speech. The gavel also fell on Ananias and Sapphira in Acts 5:9-10. Peter merely spoke and they died. He pronounced the judgement of God on them and it happened immediately. The gift of the working of miracles acts fast. This is why Jesus said His servants should not curse.

God designed this gift for the administration of discipline so that His own church will remain pure and undefiled.

> *The Apostles performed many miraculous signs and wonders among the people. And all the believers used to meet together in Solomon's colonnade. No one else dared join them, even though they were highly regarded by the people.* (Acts 5:12-13)

All those who could have defiled the Church had a change of mind when they saw what God did. A contrary person who is not ready to change cannot stay in the Church of God for long, and those who are willing to do the will of God cannot be kept away.

This gift helps to win souls. Check the next verse:

> *Nevertheless more and more men and women believed in the Lord and were added to their number.* (Acts 5:14)

The gift of the working of miracles is a showcase of God's glory and brings fear on unbelievers. One example is recorded in Luke:

> *So afterwards Jesus went to a town called Nain and his disciples and a large crowd went along with him. As he approached the town gate, a dead person was being carried out—the only son of his mother and she was a widow. And a large crowd from the town was with her. When the Lord saw her, his heart went out to her and he said, "Don't cry." Then he went up and touched the coffin and those carrying it stood still. He said, "Young man, I say to you get up!" The dead man sat up and began to talk and Jesus gave him back to his mother. They were all filled with awe and praised God. "A great prophet has appeared among us," they said. "God has come to help his people."* (Luke 7:11-16)

Any time there is a miracle, fear falls on the unbelievers and those who believe God glorify Him.

The demonstration of the supremacy of God over human limitations is another purpose of the gift. It shows people that God can do anything. Lazarus' resurrection from the dead provides a classical example:

> *Then Jesus said, "Did I not tell you that if you believed you would see the glory of God?"* (John 11:40)

No one could have thought that Lazarus would live again, but nothing is ever too late for God. After the stone had been rolled away, Jesus Christ simply beckoned Lazarus back to the land of the living.

qualifications for the gift

Three important things must be present in the lives of those who want the gifts of the working of miracles. First, If you have the gift of the working of miracles, it implies that you are working hand in hand with God, which makes you Satan's number one enemy. So if you want the gift of the working of miracles, you must be bold and fearless. Once you receive this gift, you are challenging Satan to battle.

Secondly, the one who wants the gift of the working of miracles must be ready to surrender all to God. If you are still clinging to anything in this world, you cannot have this gift. Anyone who wants to fight this battle must be ready to face any consequences and fight to the finish. With this type of determination, Satan will flee from you.

Thirdly, anyone who wants this gift must be totally dedicated. You cannot afford to be easily discouraged; you cannot fight a little and then run away. For example, Elisha was fearless. When Naaman, the commander of the Syrian army, came looking for him, Elisha knew that a great warrior was standing outside his door but he was not afraid. He did not even bother with civilities. The prophet simply sent him instructions through a messenger and did not personally attend to him. Elisha was not afraid of anybody.

> *"By all means go," the king replied. "I will send a letter to the king of Israel." So Naaman left, taking with him ten talents of silver, six thousand shekels of gold and ten sets of clothing. The letter that he took to the king of Israel read: "With this letter I am sending my servant Naaman to you so that you may cure him of his leprosy." As soon as the king of Israel read the letter he tore his robes and said, "Am I God? Can I kill and bring back to life? Why does this fellow send someone to me to be cured of his leprosy? See how he is trying to pick a quarrel with me!"* (2 Kings 5:5-7)

The king of Syria was one of the most powerful kings at this time and Naaman was the captain of his army. Naaman went to the king of Israel with a letter demanding that Naaman be healed of leprosy. The king of Israel felt it was a ploy to start another war against Israel. However, when the matter reached the man of God it became an entirely different story:

> *So Naaman went with his chariots and horses and stopped at the door of Elisha's house. Elisha sent a messenger to say to him: "Go wash yourself seven times in the Jordan and your flesh will be restored and you will be cleansed." But Naaman went away angry and said, "I thought that he would surely come out to me and stand and call on the name of the Lord his God, wave his hand over the spot and cure me of my leprosy."* (2 Kings 5:9-11)

Elisha was at home lounging while Naaman was nursing a bruised ego. He eventually wanted his healing enough to obey.

The grand slaughter of Goliath was a big miracle. David would never have succeeded had he been afraid. God has not given us the spirit of fear but power, love and a sound mind.

Elisha had surrendered all to follow Elijah, and he never looked back. He was also very dedicated. Three times Elijah tried to send him away, but he could not be dissuaded. Anyone who wants the gift must not be satisfied with the ordinary. He or she must want as much as God can give. When Elijah gave Elisha the opportunity to ask for a parting gift, Elisha asked for a double portion of the Spirit of God in Elijah. He was not content with Elijah's spiritual stature. So he asked for a double anointing and got what he wanted.

How to use the gift

When you have the gift of the working of miracles, you must be very careful because it is the most powerful gift of all. You must never use it for show or to make money. That's not the purpose of God.

When it comes to raising the dead, you must ask to know the age of' the dead person before you pray for the corpse to rise. If the fellow is already elderly, I believe you should allow him to go. If he is young, you must check with God first to learn whether He wants the person to come back to life. This is to avoid raising up someone who has already gone to Heaven. You wouldn't want to raise someone who might backslide and go to hell thereafter.

This gift must be used judiciously. Jesus did not raise everyone who died. He raised only three people: Lazarus, Jairus' daughter and the son of the widow of Nain. He could have raised several thousand but He knew what He was doing. You must find out from the Lord what He wants you to do with the gift.

Once you have permission to use this gift, it is better to work alone and undisturbed. If you read the examples of those who were raised from the dead, the person whom God used always demanded privacy. Elijah was alone with the widow's son in Zarephath.

Elisha was alone with the child of the Shunamite woman. Peter was alone with Dorcas. This is to eliminate all doubts that could hinder you when you pray the prayer of faith.

Occasionally the Spirit of God may direct you to use your body as a physical conduit for the healing virtue to flow, instead of just speaking. The body contact must not exceed three times. If nothing happens after the third time, then perhaps God does not want the miracle done.

chapter 15

The Manifestation
of the Holy Spirit

The Kingdom of God Has Already Begun

A long time ago before Jesus Christ was born, a king had a frightening dream. He was a heathen, yet God wanted him to know the meaning of the dream.

> *You looked O king and there before you stood a large statue—an enormous dazzling statue, awesome in appearance. The head of the statue was made of pure gold, its chest and arms of silver, its belly and thighs of bronze, its legs of iron, its feet partly of iron and partly of baked clay. While you were watching, a rock was cut out but not by the human hands. It struck the statue on its feet of iron and clay and smashed them.*
>
> (Daniel 2:31-34)

By the time the king woke up in the morning, he had forgotten the dream. He threatened to kill all the wise men in his kingdom if they did not tell him the dream and its interpretation. The wise men said they could not interpret a dream they did not know.

Daniel served the Living God. He said he would go and ask his God, who knows everything, about the dream and its interpretation. Daniel went to God and God told him. What is relevant to us is this:

> *Just as you saw that the feet and toes were partly of baked clay and partly of iron, so this will be a divided kingdom; yet it will have some of the strength of iron in it, even as you saw iron mixed with clay. As the toes were partly iron and partly clay so this kingdom will be partly strong and partly brittle. And just as you saw the iron mixed with baked clay so the people will be a mixture and will not remain united any more than iron mixes with clay. In the time of those kings, the God of heaven will set up a kingdom that will never be destroyed nor will it be left to another people. It will crush all those kingdoms and bring them to an end but it will itself endure forever.* (Daniel 2:41-44)

The kingdom under reference here is God's kingdom. Today there are countries called "super powers," and others that are very weak. God said this would mark the end of the age. In other words, when this time comes, we can be sure that the kingdom of God has begun.

The Bible also tells us about a prophecy concerning the End Time:

> *For to us a child is born, to us a son is given and the government will be on his shoulders. And he will be called Wonderful Counselor, Mighty God, Everlasting Father, Prince of Peace. Of the increase of his government and peace there will be no end. He will reign on David's throne and over his kingdom, establishing and upholding it with justice and righteousness from that time on and forever. The zeal of the Lord Almighty will accomplish this.* (Isaiah 9:6-7)

In other words, the kingdom of God would begin when a virgin conceives and gives birth to a child whose name would be called Jesus. John the Baptist went around spreading the news of repentance because the kingdom of God was already in their midst. Jesus Christ said the actual establishment of that kingdom was going to happen extremely close to the time of His departure from the earth:

> *And he said to them, "I tell you the truth, some who are standing here will not taste death before they see the kingdom of God come with power."* (Mark 9:1)

Just before Jesus left His disciples, they asked Him about the kingdom of God. He said the essence of the kingdom is not in its time but in the demonstration of its power. So He promised them power when the Holy Spirit came upon them. In other words, the kingdom of God was established on this earth on the day of Pentecost. When the Holy Ghost came, the disciples did receive power from the Almighty God. The Holy Ghost has been with us ever since.

Those who want to be rulers in the Kingdom of God must be baptized in the Holy Spirit. This is the only condition, because the kingdom of God is the kingdom of power.

> *For the kingdom of God is not a matter of talk but of power.* (1 Corinthians 4:20)

Only those who have spiritual power, which comes only from the Holy Spirit, can rule in the kingdom of God. The Lord said:

> *So he said to me, "This is the word of the Lord to Zerubbabel: 'Not by might nor by power but by my Spirit' says the Lord Almighty."* (Zechariah 4:6)

As soon as you are born-again, you are already seeing the kingdom of God. However, it is one thing to see the kingdom and another thing to partake in it.

god's kingdom truly rules over the world

But to those whom God has called, both Jews and Greeks, Christ the power of God and the wisdom of God. (1 Corinthians 1:24)

Anybody who has Jesus Christ has no excuse for being powerless, because He is the power of God. We have already learnt that the Holy Spirit is the power of Christ. As a ruler in the kingdom of God, you must demonstrate power, wherever you go. Paul said:

My message and my preaching were not with wise and persuasive words, but with a demonstration of the Spirit's power. (1 Corinthians 2:4)

You must demonstrate the power you have. It is visible anywhere the Gospel of Jesus Christ is preached and sinners become born-again. Paul said:

I am not ashamed of the Gospel because it is the power of God for the salvation of everyone who believes; first for the Jew, then for the Gentile. For in the Gospel a righteousness of God is revealed, a righteousness that is by faith from first to last, just as it is written: "The righteous shall live by faith." (Romans 1:16-17)

In the secular world, convicts are imprisoned not only for punishment but also for corrective purposes. However, it has been found that a lot of them become more hardened in prison. This means that the power of government institutions cannot transform people. It is the power of God that transforms people. Those of us who are born-again know that something powerful touched us and we became different when we gave our lives to Christ. When Jesus Christ comes into your life, He makes you a new creation.

If you have preached to people and they did not become believers, it may be that no power flowed from your lips. However, the power will accompany your words when you become baptized in the Holy Spirit. You will then say the same things you said before, but those who had shunned you will begin to cry under the power of conviction before you are done speaking. Those who are in the kingdom of God are the real rulers of this world. The youngest Christian who is baptized in the Holy Spirit is stronger than any president. A young Christian can change the president's decree on his or her knees.

The Bible states that God will make sinners submit to us by demonstrating His power.

> *I will not venture to speak of anything except what Christ has accomplished through me in leading the Gentiles to obey God by what I have said and done—by the power of signs and miracles, through the power of the Spirit. So from Jerusalem all the way around to Illyricum, I have fully proclaimed the gospel of Christ.*
> (Romans 15:18-19)

Paul was a man filled with the power of God. He would speak for a few minutes and miracles, signs and wonders would happen. Multitudes submitted to him.

our god is a god of signs and wonders

The Bible states that we must put on the whole armor of God. An armor is the tool of a soldier, thus there are no civilians in the kingdom of God. Our commander-in-chief is Jesus Christ. He issued a command in Matthew:

> *As you go, preach this message: The kingdom of Heaven is near. Heal the sick, raise the dead, cleanse those who have leprosy, drive out demons. Freely you have received, freely give.* (Matthew 10:7-8)

Wherever we go, we are to preach the Gospel. Every other thing Jesus wants us to do has been clearly defined. We are to obey all the commandments. Many of us obey only part of the entire code, that is, preaching the Gospel only. You cannot obey these orders on your own. You need power to perform signs and wonders.

The directive from God is that we should perform signs and wonders. He assured us that He would supply all the resources we need to do so.

> He said to them, "Go into all the world and preach the good news to all creation. Whoever believes and is baptized will be saved but whoever does not believe will be condemned. And these signs will accompany those who believe: In my name they will drive out demons; they will speak in new tongues; they will pick up snakes with their hands and when they drink deadly poison it will not hurt them at all; they will get well." After the Lord Jesus had spoken to them, he was taken up into heaven and he sat at the right hand of God. Then the disciples went out and preached everywhere and the Lord worked with them and confirmed his word by the signs that accompanied it. (Mark 16:15-20)

As soon as Jesus Christ gave the orders, the disciples went from place to place. The Lord was with them, and miracles happened. God is no respecter of persons. What He has done for others, He will do for you.

If you are not born-again, you cannot even sneak a peek at the kingdom, let alone go there, but you can make a decision to surrender to Jesus Christ today. If you are already born-again, ask God for His power.

chapter 16

The Holy spirit and joy

when the Holy spirit manifests, light is born

Whenever the Holy Spirit-filled children of God are preaching or witnessing, people always become born-again. When people become born-again, it means that light has been born. God is Light and His children are automatically lights too. Whenever there is light, there is joy.

> *Every good and perfect gift is from above coming down from the Father of the heavenly lights, who does not change like shifting shadows.* (James 1:17)

Jesus Christ is the Father of lights who brings other people into the Light.

> *In him was life and that life was the light of men. The light shines in the darkness but the darkness has not understood it. The true light that gives light to every man was coming into the world.* (John 1: 4-5,9)

How did Jesus Christ come into the world? An angel told Mary that she was going to have a baby. Mary felt this was impossible because she was a virgin and not yet married. The angel told her that the Holy Ghost would overshadow her, and Mary got her miracle through the Holy Ghost. We are in the dispensation of the Holy Ghost. All those who have lived before us are inferior to us. We are the ones living in the time of power.

How are you going to get your miracle? It is through the Holy Spirit. How are you going to be healed? Through the Holy Spirit. How will your impossibilities become possibilities? How will your sorrow become joy? How can your darkness become Light? Everything happens through the Holy Spirit, which on the day of Pentecost came in like a mighty rushing wind.

If the Holy Spirit is moving, there will always be joy and miracles. In Acts 3:1-8 we find the story of the healing of the lame man through Peter. The lame man was able to walk again through the Holy Spirit inside Peter that flowed into him when Peter pulled him up on his feet. The man followed Peter and John into the church joyously. Here is another example of a joyous event:

> *Philip went down to a city in Samaria and proclaimed the Christ there. When the crowds heard Philip and saw the miraculous signs he did, they all paid close attention to what he said. With shrieks, evil spirits came out of many and many paralytics and cripples were healed. So there was great joy in that city.*
>
> (Acts 8:5-8)

Because the Holy Spirit moved, miracles happened and there was joy. We can get the Holy Spirit to move by rejoicing. If there is joy, the Holy Spirit will move. When the Holy Spirit moves, there will be miracles. When there are miracles, there will be joy. If we want the Holy Spirit to be in perpetual manifestation in our midst, we must rejoice perpetually.

When Joshua came against the wall of Jericho, God instructed him to tell the people to shout for joy. They shouted, the Holy Spirit moved and the wall fell. (Joshua 6:15-16) When some kings came against Jehoshaphat, God told him not to fight but to rejoice and sing. When the army sang, the Holy Spirit moved and miracles occurred. The enemies began to kill themselves. (2 Chr. 20:21-22)

The best way to drive away your enemy is by praising the enemy of your enemy. If you want to drive away an enemy of God, all you have to do is to praise God.

You may say you know a lot about joy; after all, the Bible states that we should rejoice always, even in the face of persecution. There was a time the Apostles were persecuted, but someone warned the persecutors not to kill them because if they truly belonged to God, they could not be destroyed.

> *His speech persuaded them. They called the apostles in and had them flogged. Then they ordered them not to speak in the name of Jesus and let them go. The apostles left the Sanhedrin, rejoicing because they had been counted worthy of suffering disgrace for the Name.*
> (Acts 5:40-41)

While hoping for a miracle, in the midst of trials and temptations, persecution and suffering, we can leave the Holy Spirit no choice but to manifest simply by rejoicing.

chapter 17

The Holy Spirit and Angels

When the Holy Spirit Moves, Angels Follow

In speaking of angels he says, "He makes his angels winds, his servants flames of fire." (Hebrews 1:7)

The Bible says angels are spirits, and there are two types: holy angels and fallen angels. The fallen are those Satan took with him when he fell. They are unholy and unclean. However, we have angels with God in Heaven who stayed loyal to God at the fall. Those are the holy angels.

In a popular cliché, birds of the same feathers always flock together. It follows therefore that whenever the Holy Spirit is moving, holy angels must follow. Anywhere the Holy Spirit is in manifestation, angels are there too. Consequently, where Holy Spirit-filled children of God are gathered rejoicing, angels abound.

What do these angels that follow the Holy Spirit do?

To which of the angels did God ever say, "Sit at my right hand until I make your enemies a footstool for your feet?" Are not angels ministering spirits sent to serve those who will inherit salvation?

(Hebrews 1:13-14)

Angels are to minister to the heirs of salvation—that is, anyone who is born-again, an heir of God Almighty. Why does the Holy Spirit go about with many servants? So they can solve our problems. It does not matter how many of us are in a congregation; the Holy Spirit has enough angels to supply the needs of everyone. Every true child of God has angelic bodyguards.

> *The angel of the Lord encamps around those who fear him and delivers them.* (Psalm 34:7)

Those who fear God are His children. We cannot see these angels unless God enables us. But before God shows you, He will make sure that you have reached a certain stage spiritually so that you do not become frightened when you see them.

These angels have instructions from Almighty God to take very good care of us. The order is such that if you knock your feet against a stone, God would query the angel in charge.

> *For he will command his angels concerning you to guard you in all your ways; they will lift you up in their hands, so that you will not strike your foot against a stone.* (Psalm 91:11-12)

The angels are also told to deal with any spiritual lions roaring against our lives. They are to handle any demonic activities designed to harm us. If you are not a child of God and you think the devil cannot hurt you, you are probably suicidal because you do not have angels taking care of you. Demons have eyes to see the angels surrounding children of God.

These angels also bring answers to our prayers:

> *While I was still in prayer, Gabriel, the man I had seen in the earlier vision, came to me in swift flight about*

the time of the evening sacrifice. He instructed me and said to me, "Daniel, I have now come to give you insight and understanding. As soon as you began to pray an answer was given which I have come to tell you for you are highly esteemed. Therefore consider the message and understand the vision." (Daniel 9:21-23)

The moment you begin to pray, God will command an angel to take the answer to you. This is why I am so sure that God will answer my prayers. When God wants to send you a message He sends it through someone that He can trust—His angels. Often human beings cannot be trusted by God. For example, once God sent me to someone and I was afraid to deliver His message. It was not until God said that if I did not deliver the message, the person would die and I would be held responsible that I delivered the message. Angels do not argue with God.

This is how the birth of Jesus Christ came about: His mother Mary was pledged to be married to Joseph, but before they came together, she was found to be with child through the Holy Spirit. Because Joseph her husband was a righteous man and did not want to expose her to public disgrace, he had in mind to divorce her quietly. But after he had considered this, an angel of the Lord appeared to him in a dream and said, "Joseph son of David, do not be afraid to take Mary home as your wife, because what is conceived in her is from the Holy Spirit." (Matthew 1:18-20)

If a prophet had been sent to Joseph, the secret would probably have been leaked to the wife of the prophet and all his friends, but the angel delivered the message and went back to Heaven. Therefore, any time God wants to tell you a special secret, He would send an angel.

Angels also warn us of dangers ahead and how to avoid them:

When they had gone, an angel of the Lord appeared to Joseph in a dream. "Get up," he said, "Take the child and his mother and escape to Egypt. Stay there until I tell you for Herod is going to search for the child to kill him." (Matthew 2:13)

Herod was planning to kill Jesus Christ but before he concluded his plot, God leaked the secret. The child he wanted to kill was already beyond his reach. The moment the agents of the devil plan against me, my Father knows and sends an angel to tell me the plan and how to avoid it.

A lot of things happen to Christians that they do not understand. For example, you may want to travel but something suddenly causes a delay. It may be the Almighty God clearing the way for you. God knows how to deliver His own.

Furthermore, it is these angels who will carry us home if we "sleep" before the rapture.

The time came when the beggar died and the angels carried him to Abraham's side. The rich man also died and was buried. (Luke 16:22)

We will have a free ride to Heaven. If we do not die before Jesus Christ comes, it is the angels who will gather us when it's time to go.

At that time the sign of the Son of Man will appear in the sky and all the nations of the earth will mourn. They will see the Son of Man coming on the clouds of the sky with power and great glory. And he will send his angels with a loud trumpet call and they will gather his elect from the four winds, from one end of the heavens to the other. (Matthew 24:30-31)

Not a single child of God will be forgotten. The angels will pick them up wherever they may be.

The Angelic Choir Never Stops Singing— why must we?

The holy angels love to sing and do so all the time. They are always singing, "Holy, Holy, Holy, Lord God Almighty." Consequently, wherever the Holy Spirit is moving, with the angels around, there is music even though we may not hear it. The music is going on constantly and it is only those who have their spiritual ears open that can hear the music.

Anyone can praise God at any time. Many particularly do when they are happy. But those who can praise God in the way He *ought* to be praised are those who are spirit-filled, who know how to praise God from their spirit.

> *God is spirit and his worshippers must worship in spirit and in truth.* (John 4:24)

We are supposed to praise God in spirit and in truth. David talks about how he praises God:

> *Seven times a day I praise you for your righteous laws.*
> (Psalm 119:164)

What inspired David to do this? God made him king over Israel, but we are greater than David is. At the Marriage of the Lamb, David will be a guest while we will be the Bride.

> *Do you get drunk on wine, which leads to debauchery. Instead be filled with the Spirit. Speak to one another with Psalms, hymns and spirituals songs. Sing and make music in your heart to the Lord. Always giving thanks to God the Father for everything, in the name of our Lord Jesus Christ.* (Ephesians 5:18-20)

Our conversations should be filled with praising the Lord. If angels, who are our servants, sing praises to God all the time, I think we should do better. It does not matter how your voice sounds, make a joyful noise to the Lord. Let it come from the bottom of your heart and it will be pleasing to Him.

chapter 18

The Holy Spirit and visions

The Holy Spirit Manifests visions

Human beings have two sets of eyes: the physical and the spiritual. In 2 Kings 6:17, when Elisha and his servant were surrounded by the Syrian army, the servant went in to ask his master what to do in the face of the siege. Elisha told him that their divine defense was more powerful than the weapons of the enemy. The servant did not understand because he could only see himself and his master against a whole army. Elisha then prayed that God would open the eyes of his servant. The Lord did and the servant saw those on their side. Physically, this servant was not blind, but he was spiritually. God opened his spiritual eyes.

There are many things that we cannot see with the physical eyes. Those with well-developed spiritual eyes are always at peace because they can see what you cannot see. With physical eyes you can see problems and difficulties, but with spiritual eyes, they can see victories.

When can one's spiritual eyes be opened? It is the Holy Spirit who gives spiritual eyes. If the eyes are closed He can open them. If they are destroyed, He can restore them. This is why Jesus Christ said:

god, the Holy spirit

He will bring glory to me by taking from what is mine and making it known to you. All that belongs to the Father is mine. That is why I said the Spirit will take from what is mine and make it known to you.

(John 16:14-15)

The Holy Spirit is the One who can show you divine things. There are several examples in the Bible of people who were filled with the Holy Spirit and who saw visions. Paul said:

I must go on boasting. Although there is nothing to be gained, I will go on to visions and revelations from the Lord. To keep me from becoming conceited because of these surpassingly great revelations, there was given to me a thorn in my flesh a messenger of Satan to torment me. (2 Corinthians 12:1,7)

These visions kept Paul going despite severe difficulties. Even if we do not see any other vision, we should be able to see our home in Heaven. If we can see it, we can keep going, whatever our problems may be. If God will show you your home in Heaven, there will be no need for anyone to preach to you.

What you fix your eyes on determines what happens to you. For example, if you are looking back, you will go back. If you always think of your old friends and all those things you did in the past that you know you cannot do anymore as a Christian, soon you will backslide. You know the story of Lot's wife. (Gen. 19:26) She looked back, and when God saw that she did not want to move on she became stuck to the ground.

If you keep your eyes on your difficulties, you will become depressed. Those who do not stop thinking about their problems never rise above them. They always sink. Remember that as long as Peter kept his eyes on Jesus he walked on water. But the minute he looked at the waves, that is, the minute he noticed he was doing something that was naturally impossible, he began to sink.

However, those who are always looking at Jesus Christ get salvation, light, joy, hope and victory.

Just as Moses lifted up the snake in the desert, so the Son of Man must be lifted up that everyone who believes in him may have eternal life. (John 3:14-15)

Those who look up to Jesus Christ always become elevated. If you want victory and glory, you must look upward.

I lift up my eyes to you, to you whose throne is in heaven. (Psalm 123:1)

Each time you look up to Heaven, you will see glory. There is no sickness in Heaven so if you are sick and you look heavenward, you can only see healing there, and you tap into it. There is no famine and unemployment there. Each time you have problems, keep your eyes in the right place.

In Acts when they were stoning Stephen, instead of looking at the crowd, he looked upwards into Heaven.

But Stephen full of the Holy Spirit looked up to heaven and saw the glory of God and Jesus standing at the right hand of God. (Acts 7:55)

Stephen looked up and saw the glory of God. Many Christians spend a lot of time looking at themselves and the situations around them. Whenever you look down, you will see defeat. Children of God are to look at the Almighty God. If you look at Him you will not be put to shame. The Bible tells us that one day we are going to see God as He is.

Now we see but a poor reflection as in a mirror; then we shall see face to face. Now I know in part, then I shall know fully even as I am fully known.
(1 Corinthians 13:12)

They will see his face and his name will be on their foreheads. (Revelation 22:4)

I am going to see God face to face. There is, however, a little condition:

Blessed are the pure in heart for they will see God.
(Matthew 5:8)

no progress without visions

We will give vision another interpretation here: the visions you can have yourself as a spirit-filled child of God rather than visions of God or angels. God made a promise that as soon as you are filled with the Spirit of God, you can begin to see visions. Joel prophesied about a promise that can never change:

And afterward I will pour out my Spirit on all people. Your sons and daughters will prophesy, your old men will dream dreams, your young men will see visions.
(Joel 2:28)

We shall see visions. We need to explain what God means here. God says:

Where there is no revelation, the people cast off restraint; but blessed is he who keeps the law.
(Proverbs 29:18)

Anytime there is no vision, there will be no progress. When there is no progress, people will eventually perish. When you want to build a house, the first thing you need is a vision of the house. You will decide what type of house you want to build. Later, you will draw your idea on paper or hire an architect. At this time, you may not have the parcel of land to build it on but you already have a vision of your house. Once the vision is there, you will work towards it.

Many people do not have a vision of what they can become. If you never dream of becoming greater than you are now, you never will. There are people that God could use mightily, people who could become world evangelists or build a hundred churches before Jesus comes. However, they never think about it. They never have visions or goals. All the great men of the Bible had mighty visions that kept them going.

> *By faith Abraham when called to go to a place he would later receive as his inheritance, obeyed and went, even though he did not know where he was going. By faith he made his home in the Promised Land like a stranger in a foreign country; he lived in tents, as did Isaac and Jacob, who were heirs with him of the same promise. For he was looking forward to the city with foundations whose architect and builder is God. By Faith Abraham, even though he was past age and Sarah herself was barren was enabled to become a father because he considered him faithful who had made the promise. And so from this one man and he as good as dead came descendants as numerous as the stars in the sky and as countless as the sand on the seashore. All these people were still living by faith when they died. They did not receive the things promised; they only saw them and welcomed them from a distance. And they admitted that they were aliens and strangers on earth. People who say such things show that they are looking for a country of their own. If they had been thinking of the country they had left, they would have had opportunity to return. Instead, they were longing for a better country, a heavenly one. Therefore God is not ashamed to be called their God for he has prepared a city for them.* (Hebrews 11:8-16)

They had a vision of a city built by God, called "The Heavenly Jerusalem," and they wanted to go there. These great men knew that a time would come when they would reach the city built for them by God. Even though they died before reaching it, you can be sure that they are resting there now.

Is it possible to have visions of material things and they materialize? In Genesis 30:25-43 we read about Jacob's employment history with Laban. Jacob worked for fourteen years for two wives. Laban would not let Jacob go. Laban asked Jacob to name his price. Jacob asked for his emoluments—any of Laban's cattle with spots or freckles. Laban accepted, thinking Jacob would be the loser. However, when the animals conceived, Jacob got some trees and made spots on them and placed them in front of the good cattle. This was so that when they delivered, the little ones would have spots and speckles. You may say this is superstitious but it is in the Bible. It is what you visualize that will manifest. All the good cattle had spots and became Jacob's.

We have another example in Genesis:

> *After this the word of the Lord came to Abram in a vision: "Do not be afraid Abram, I am your shield and very great reward." But Abram said, "O Sovereign Lord what can you give me since I remain childless and the one who will inherit my estate is Eliezer of Damascus?" And Abram said, "You have given me no children; so a servant in my household will be my heir." Then the word of the Lord came to him: "This man will not be your heir, but a son coming from your own body will be your heir." He took him outside and said, "Look up at the heavens and count the stars—if indeed you can count them." Then he said to him, "So shall your offspring be."*
>
> (Genesis 15:1-5)

God brought Abraham out to count the stars as an example of how numerous his children would be. At the time, Abraham had no children but from then on, any time he looked at the stars he visualized them. He is not alive today but how many children belong to Abraham? Zillions of them. Every Christian is of the seed of Abraham.

If you are barren, why don't you practice visualizing yourself holding a baby? Visualize people coming in to congratulate you. Visualize yourself testifying to many people about the birth of your baby, glorifying God. Dream big. Our God is a big God and there is nothing impossible for Him.

chapter 19

when the Holy spirit moves

Jesus promised that the Holy Spirit will show us things to come:

I have much to say to you more than you can now bear.
But when He the Spirit of Truth comes He will guide
you into all Truth. He will not speak on his own; He will
speak only what He hears and He will tell you what is
yet to come. (John 16:12-13)

The Holy Spirit will show me what is to come. If you can tune your frequency to that of the Holy Spirit, He will show you, too, in details. Jesus spoke many times to His disciples in proverbs. He said there would be a time when He would no more speak in proverbs. (John 16:25) I believe the time has come when God will speak plainly.

"Prophecy" simply means what God is saying about a particular situation. God can tell you many things plainly. He can tell you whom to marry, what to buy, which direction to go. If you learn how to listen to the Holy Spirit, He will show you things to come.

when the Holy spirit moves in, Demons move out

God is Light. When light comes in, darkness must depart. Demons are forces of darkness. Consequently, whenever the Holy Spirit moves in, demons must move out.

> *Philip went down to a city in Samaria and proclaimed the Christ there. When the crowds heard Philip and saw the miraculous signs he did, they all paid close attention to what he said. With shrieks, evil spirits came out of many and many paralytics and cripples were healed. So there was great joy in that city.*
>
> (Acts 8:5-8)

Anywhere the Spirit of God is moving, demons must leave. You do not have to beg them to go; it is their duty to obey the voice of the Lord.

> *Once when we were going to the place of prayer, we were met by a slave girl who had a spirit by which she predicted the future. She earned a great deal of money for her owners by fortune telling. This girl followed Paul and the rest of us, shouting, "These men are servants of the Most High God, who are telling you the way to be saved. She kept this up for many days. Finally Paul became so troubled that he turned around and said to the spirit, "In the name of Jesus Christ I command you to come out of her!" At that moment the spirit left her.* (Acts 16:16-18)

Other people were using this girl. She did not want to be a soothsayer but her masters compelled her. Paul made it very easy for God to set her free. There are some adults who deliberately want to hold on to forces of darkness. Unless they voluntarily let go, your prayers may not have the necessary power to make the evil spirits leave.

There are some brethren who spend time talking with demons in the name of praying or deliverance sessions. They always quote Matthew to support why they do this:

> *When he arrived at the other side in the region of the Gadarenes, two demon-possessed men coming from the tombs met him. They were so violent that no one could pass that way. "What do you want with us, Son of God?" they shouted. "Have you come here to torture us before the appointed time?" Some distance from them a large herd of pigs was feeding. The demons begged Jesus, "If you drive us out, send us into the herd of pigs." He said to them, "Go!" So they came out and went into the pigs and the whole herd rushed down the steep bank into the lake and died in the water.*
>
> (Matthew 8:28-32)

There were two mad people who were so terrible that everyone avoided them, but Jesus Christ was not afraid of them because they recognized Him as the Son of God. Demons should recognize you as a child of God. The demons were afraid of Jesus Christ. If you are a true child of God, forces of darkness should be afraid of you. Every true child of God must be a source of danger to the devil. You should not be running away from them; they should be the ones running away from you.

You are to cast out demons and not to talk to them or beg them to go. Some people say they do not want to cast out demons from others because they do not want to be possessed themselves. How can you be possessed if you are covered in the Blood of the Lamb? If you are covered with the Blood of Jesus Christ, no demon can cross that bloodline. If he does, he will become born-again. Since the devil does not want to become born-again, he will not attempt to possess you if you are covered with the Blood of Jesus Christ. No demon can usurp the Holy Spirit's residence. It is demons that leave for the Holy Spirit to come in.

special miracles belong to special people

A miracle is something special, therefore *special* miracles are extraordinary occurrences. Whenever the Holy Spirit is at work, extra special things happen. Many people do not need miracles and some people do not need ordinary things, but they need something very special. This passage explains my kind of special miracles:

> *Nevertheless more and more men and women believed in the Lord and were added to their number. As a result people brought the sick into the streets and laid them on beds and mats so that at least Peter's shadow might fall on some of them as he passed by. Crowds gathered also from the towns around Jerusalem, bringing their sick and those tormented by evil spirits and all of them were healed.* (Acts 5:14-16)

I want you to imagine what happened here. Sick people were brought out for Peter's shadow to heal them. You may say this happened in the olden days, but it can still happen today. Jesus has not changed. The Holy Spirit has not changed. He is still performing those miracles today.

> *God did extraordinary miracles through Paul so that even handkerchiefs and aprons that had touched him were taken to the sick and their illnesses were cured and the evil spirits left them.* (Acts 19:11-12)

God did special things through Paul that can still happen today. Some years ago, on my way from the United States where I had seen God perform some miracles, I talked to Him about those miracles and told Him that if He did not do them in Nigeria then He was partial. He started giving us opportunities that showed He is the same everywhere. I was in my office one sunny day when a woman came to see me about her sister's strange sickness. I told her to bring the patient but she said her sister would not come. So

I told her to get a handkerchief and we prayed over it. Word got back to us that the sick sister was given the handkerchief and she became healed.

You may not need anything materially, but God can give you so much power that you too can pray on handkerchiefs and send them to the sick so they are healed. Although Jesus Christ did not heal with handkerchiefs or His shadow, He said we would do greater works than He did.

chapter 20

The Holy Spirit and Fear

Under normal circumstances, fear is not a positive thing. When a man is gripped with fear, he begins to behave in an abnormal way. He may run when nobody is chasing him, or may live in a secured house yet be unable to sleep because of fear. This negative type of fear is not for children of God. He has not given us the spirit of bondage to fear. We are His children and not slaves.

Holy fear is when you fear God. There is only One you need to fear, in Heaven and on earth: Jesus Christ.

> *The Lord Almighty is the One you are to regard as holy, he is the One you are to fear, he is the One you are to dread.* (Isaiah 8:13)

Once you fear God the way He should be feared, you will discover that all other fears will disappear. Look at what Jesus Christ said:

> *Do not be afraid of those who kill the body but cannot kill the soul. Rather be afraid of the One who can destroy both soul and body in hell.* (Matthew 10:28)

If you fear God, there is no reason why you should fear human beings. First, if God is for you, nobody can be against you. If God is on your side, it will not matter if the whole world comes against you because they will all fail. And if you do not fear God, you are bound to fear something. You will fear the devil and demonic activities.

Let's assume the opposition can kill you, but if they do, they are only speeding you on to Heaven. If God were to show you what awaits you in Heaven, you will not want to stay here, but you cannot kill yourself to get to Heaven. Thus whoever kills you here is merely helping you.

Do not fear those who can kill the body but cannot kill the soul. There is someone who can kill the body and throw the soul into Hell; this is the One you must fear. When we talk about the fear of God, it is not the type of fear that you feel when you see a snake. It is mixed with love. The foundation for the fear of God is the love of God. In other words, the fear of God is reverence for Him.

When you love and adore someone and they love you in return, you will not want to do anything to offend them.

> *And now O Israel, what does the Lord your God ask of you but to fear the Lord your God, to walk in all his ways to love him, to serve the Lord your God with all your heart and with all your soul.*
>
> (Deuteronomy 10:12)

You are to fear God with a fear born out of love

> *It is the Lord your God you must follow and Him you must revere. Keep his commands and obey Him; serve Him and hold fast to him.* (Deuteronomy 13:4)

How can you cleave to someone you are afraid of? Love settles this dilemma.

When some Christians sin, they become afraid of punishment and run away from God. How can you run away from your Father? If you have offended Him, go back to Him and plead with Him. If He has to knock you on the head, take the knock and resolve everything. If you run away from God, you will run into the hands of the devil. I prefer God's punishment to being Satan's friend. When the devil says he loves you, he is planning to kill you.

Any time the Holy Spirit is in action, particularly when He decides to judge or expose sinners, fear abounds. This is the type of fear that recognizes God as both a loving Father and a strict disciplinarian.

> *When Ananias heard this, he fell down and died. And*
> *great fear seized all who heard what had happened.*
> (Acts 5:5)

The fear of the Holy Spirit sifts the grain from the chaff as pretenders run away from Church while earnest seekers of the truth of God troop in.

godly fear and godly service are linked

If you really want to follow God and serve Him the way you ought to, you must fear Him.

> *He would plunge it into the pan or kettle or caldron or*
> *pot and the priest would take for himself whatever the*
> *fork brought up. This is how they treated all the*
> *Israelites who came to Shiloh.* (1 Samuel 2:14)

If you say you serve God and you do not fear Him, you are a liar. If you don't fear Him, you will disobey Him. As Christians, we do not do certain things, not for fear of our pastor but because we know God sees us. If you remove the fear of God from the life of any man, there is nothing he will not do. Anyone who follows God will not do evil.

*Now fear the Lord and serve him with all faithfulness.
Throw away the gods your father worshipped beyond
the River and in Egypt and serve the Lord.*

(Joshua 24:14)

You can serve Him in sincerity and in truth, if only you fear Him.
When there is no fear, there will be no discipline. If you want people to be disciplined, introduce them to the fear of God. It is the
beginning of wisdom. When you fear God, you will be wise.

*Now all has been heard, here is the conclusion of the
matter; Fear God and keep His commandments for this
is the whole duty of man.* (Ecclesiastes 12:13)

All you need to do is fear God. Obey Him and every other thing will
fall into place.

men and houses of god should be reverenced too

Anything belonging to God must be treated with reverence. This
includes His sanctuary and all men of God living according to the
truth of God, who must be held in high esteem because they represent God.

*He who receives you receives me and he who receives
me receives the one who sent me.* (Matthew 10:40)

You can see the automatic linkages here. If you dishonor the rep-
resentatives of God you dishonor God. A pastor represents God all
the time, so you had better honor Him because you honor God.

In Exodus we see the way the men in Moses' era treated him as a
representative of God:

*And whenever Moses went out to the tent, all the peo-
ple rose and stood at the entrances of their tents,*

watching Moses until he entered the tent.

(Exodus 33:8)

Just as the people respected Moses, you are to honor men of God not for their own sake, but for the sake of God whom they represent. This is probably why men of God are called "Reverend." You are to honor the house of God, too.

> *Observe my Sabbaths and have reverence for my Sanctuary. I am the Lord.* (Leviticus 19:30)

We must respect anything that belongs to God. Doing this attracts blessings.

god rewards those who fear him

Let's take a look at some of the things that will be ours if we fear God and respect everything that belongs to Him.

> *Who then is the man that fears the Lord? He will instruct him in the way chosen for him.* (Psalm 25:12)

If you need day to day direction from God, all you need to do is fear Him.

> *How great is your goodness which you have stored for those who fear you, which you bestow in the sight of men on those who take refuge in you.* (Psalm 31:19)

God rewards those who fear Him with mighty goodness and mercy.

> *His mercy extends to those who fear him from generation to generation.* (Luke 1:50)

The mercy of God is for those who fear God. It will take us to Heaven. If God were to judge us based on our history, we would all be chairpersons in hell. If you want to be a favorite bride of God, what you must do is this:

> *Then Peter began to speak, I now realize how true it is that God does not show favoritism. But accepts men from every nation who fear him and do what is right.*
> (Acts 10:34-35)

Those who refuse to become born again do so because they do not fear God. If you have been in this position up until now, I appeal to you to surrender your life to Jesus Christ. Fear God and seek your salvation and He will bless you.

about the author

Enoch Adejare Adeboye became the General Overseer of The Redeemed Christian Church of God in 1981. The church has experienced unprecedented growth since he became its spiritual and administrative head. Under his leadership, the church hosts a monthly prayer vigil on the first Friday of every month at the headquarters in the Redemption Camp, on the outskirts of Lagos, Nigeria, attracting about 500,000 people per session. Similar meetings are held bi-annually in the United Kingdom and the United States, where the Church has a strong presence.

Also in the eighties, God led Pastor Adeboye to establish "model parishes" that continue to bring young people into the Kingdom in large numbers. The church now has over two million members in about four thousand parishes all over the world.

Pastor Adeboye, a mathematician who holds a Ph.D. in hydrodynamics, lectured at the University of Lagos, Nigeria for many years. He is also a prolific writer of many titles used by God to touch lives. He is married to Pastor Foluke Adeboye and they are blessed with four children.